A SCHOOL FOR EVERYONE

Design for a Middle, Junior, or Senior High School That Combines the Old and the New

by WITHDRAWN
J. Lloyd Trump

THE NATIONAL ASSOCIATION OF SECONDARY SCHOOL PRINCIPALS
RESTON, VA.

Copyright 1977

THE NATIONAL ASSOCIATION
OF SECONDARY SCHOOL PRINCIPALS
1904 Association Dr., Reston, Va. 22091

ISBN 0-88210-077-7
Library of Congress Catalog Card Number: 77-73036

Contents

Introduction

This book has a positive, constructive theme: it is about a school for everyone!

The contents are not merely repetitive statements of my earlier publications in the 1950s and 1960s. What some persons labeled as "the Trump plan" had its place in schools that sought ways to break conventional, uniform policies and procedures. Those efforts helped point the way to better designs. Too often, however, the changes became ends in themselves even though evaluations showed positive effects.

The design described in this book incorporates experiences of the past eight years in a Model Schools Project, called "Schools of Tomorrow," sponsored by the National Association of Secondary School Principals [NASSP]. This longitudinal undertaking, partly financed by the Danforth Foundation, involved at various times 34 junior and senior high schools. They were large and small, they were located in cities and smaller places, they were public and private, to name only a few of the variables. The present design, however, differs somewhat from the model in that project.

The NASSP over the years has issued a number of major statements as guidelines for improving schools. This book translates many of them into a workable model. Chapters 1 and 2 give the rationale; 3, 4, and 5 describe the people involved; 6 through 14 show various program aspects; 15 through 19 indicate priorities and procedures for making the changes; and 20 presents the total plan for the school with some future agendas.

Although the subtitle specifies middle, junior, and senior high schools, I believe the design with minor modifications is also appropriate in elementary schools. After all, the kindergarten is conventionally the most individualized time for pupils in schools!

This book is for everybody concerned about more effective schools. Whether one's interests are in a large city, a small town, or a medium-sized place, regardless of financial conditions, population problems, or other pressures, this book shows the reader how to provide better schools for everyone by breaking through the restrictions of many existing standard policies and procedures.

Going beyond the provision of simplistic recipes that anyone may follow blindly, the emphasis here is on alternatives that creative persons can use to improve any school. At the end of each chapter there are suggestions on how to start.

J.L.T.

Rationale for Improvement

Schools can be better than they are. The programs that conventional schools provide today serve some individuals reasonably well; other persons need quite different arrangements. The school set forth in this book is for *all* students, teachers, and supervisor-managers.

1

Who and Why?

Who shall speak for education? Whom shall we be-lieve and why? Who should determine what changes, if any, are to be made in a given school? What new directions do the times suggest? Why are different designs necessary?

TODAY'S schools have both problems and critics. That situation is not new. Only the quantity and urgency are more pronounced.

Suspending students, forcing dropouts, dismissing teachers, filing grievances, and calling strikes may be necessary at times but they are expressions of frustrations rather than constructive solutions to deeper problems.

The need is for constructive alternatives. The design presented in this book for a secondary school—middle, junior, or senior high—enables everyone in it to attain success and to have personal satisfactions. Such goals require approaches to schooling different from both conventional school programs and fragmented educational innovations.

What is needed is a school that offers a variety of choices with appropriate guidance and controls. Its program must emphasize the motivation, background, and opportunities that everyone needs to choose wisely among the available options. School policies also must permit participants to change their minds as added experiences provide bases for better choices.

Such a design avoids the fetish of uniformity that often plagues today's schools. Although new developments are essential, conventional programs are offered, too, but they are enriched by numerous variables.

The chapters that follow show how the school develops the maximum potential of each student, teacher, and supervisory-management team member. Also indicated are unconventional methods for evaluating individual productivity and the quality of the school program.

To Whom It May Concern

This book is for many people. Students need to understand how schools can change to serve their needs more productively. Since teachers have crucial roles in the change process, they need to perceive more clearly what their functions should be. The same is true for those who supervise and manage the enterprise.

The school involves many other persons who are involved in the control of policies, finances, and evaluations. University professors who prepare teachers, work with the products of the schools, develop materials, serve as consultants, and perform other services for the schools need to comprehend what has to be done to improve schools. There are implications, too, for persons who plan and build schools and for others who provide school supplies, equipment, transportation, and other physical arrangements. Some have financial interests in the process; some do not.

The point is that in this society, education truly is a wide concern. This book is addressed to everyone; to whom it may concern is you, whoever you are.

The design here is for schools in any kind of locale: inner-city, small town, big town, suburbia. Teaching and learning operate from the same basic premises, regardless of the age of the learners or where they live. The differences among schools are a matter of degree.

Efforts to improve schools cannot exclude any place where teaching and learning occur. To do so is to treat the subject inadequately. Many things that students learn about life are taught outside the school—in homes, the streets, and elsewhere by persons who have little or no systematic preparation for teaching. Racism, sexism, and drug dependence unfortunately are remembered better than what students learn in school. The mass media are also powerful teachers. School professionals need to analyze and utilize constructively the varied sources of learning experiences.

This book is about the improvement of teaching and learning in all places. The aim is to clarify not only what belongs in *schools* but also what needs to happen in *homes* and in the *community*. Confusion abounds regarding the potential in each of these three environments. The result may be irresponsible use of the three, unreasonable lack of coordination, and ineffective coping with the differences among schools, homes, and communities.

Who Wants To Change What?

Some people answer that question by saying, "As little as possible" or "Whatever will do the most good." Both answers are reasonable as well as popular. Possibly a more basic question is: *Who* wants *what* changed and *why?* The desire for change almost always is highly personal since it relates to something that an individual or an organized group does not like for some specific reason.

A parent wishes to change a school program because a son or daughter is not succeeding in the existing program. A taxpayer wishes to modify the schools because they cost too much. An employer wishes to change the schools because employees lack specific training or attitudes. A professor wishes to change schools because few students are interested or adequately prepared in the professor's specialty.

Students, too, wish to change the program for many reasons—they are bored, believe they are working too hard, feel they are unchallenged, consider the material irrelevant, or do not like a teacher.

Organized groups pressure for what they define as basic education, more attention to the free enterprise system, more favorable attitudes towards organized labor, the capitalist system, conservation of resources, and a host of other special concerns.

Some changes are forced for unrelated reasons such as a financial crisis that cuts budgets with no specific goals other than "spend less."

Professional educators, therefore, need to listen to critics and to analyze forces, because every criticism has the potential for stimulating change. Even more important, the educator needs to help perturbed people understand the ramifications that their concerns hold for school improvement. Negative criticism may be as useful as positive criticism. Even national interests of the moment can be channeled by the school to improve the program.

Kinds of Change

Persons who want to improve schools immediately confront a dilemma. A reasonable approach to improving a program is to analyze first what needs to be done. But who and what determine priorities?

Some proposals are narrow and oversimplified. For example, few gains result when flexible scheduling merely redistributes time into three days a week instead of five, with some periods longer than others, if the school does not change its curriculum, methods of teaching, and a number of other conventional features. Likewise, changing the grading system merely for the sake of change is pointless. A pass-fail system is less descriptive than A B C D F.

Developing learning packages without changing the curriculum produces few gains. Also, a continuous progress program is essential for each student to go at a personal pace. Even continuous progress is not beneficial if the school does not reexamine its curriculum. The point is that change may be merely in form and not in substance with only superficial attention to the results produced.

Raising teachers' salaries enables teachers to live better and to have more pride in their work, but does it improve their methods of teaching? Building a new school may enhance pride in the community and provide a more pleasant and healthful environment for students, but does it improve the quality of education?

Interestingly enough, one common approach to changing schools has been quite successful—the introduction of extracurricular activities. Providing a variety of clubs, athletic activities, assembly programs, special contests, student government activities, special drives and participation in community events, and a host of other programs enriches the curriculum. However, many students do not participate in these activities, particularly those from less affluent homes and with poor scholastic achievement and attendance.

These activities do not replace or alter the curriculum; they are additional events, mostly elective, designed especially to meet current student and faculty interests and needs. Many students believe they derive more benefits from extracurricular activities than from the regular school programs. Some teachers concur. Consider, however, that if school programs were enriched, the need for extracurricular activities would diminish or possibly disappear because what is now achieved only by them would be accomplished in the total, more flexible program.

Changes in schools may be small or large, fragmentary or comprehensive. Small changes are soporific. Massive changes are dramatic. Partial changes bring pleasant feelings and create a community image of a school that continuously seeks better ways of doing things.

Total change develops an image of revolution rather than evolution. Gains from partial change are minimal; the potential of total change is maximal. Thus, we have dilemmas which by definition are not solvable. How the school leadership works with these situations and plans accordingly is the subject of this book.

A variety of pressure groups operate both to change and to maintain the *status quo*. Most opposition to improving schools is based upon inadequate information about purposes, programs, and evaluations. It is essential that everyone understands the reasons and procedures for making schools more relevant and adaptable to the needs of students, teachers, and supervisors-managers. The goal has to be increased sharing of information, not seeking power by controlling information.

Schools also need to involve professional help much more than they do now, including the help of researchers. One reason educational research has had relatively little impact on schools is that many of these experts have been too far removed from everyday school operations. Members of the American Educational Research Association do sophisticated research and present their reports at annual meetings and in publications. The problem is they communicate mostly with other researchers.

Researchers must learn to communicate their findings to practitioners. More of them need to work for extended periods of time in schools as researchers-in-residence. The manifold interactions in the setting will help everyone. Both university graduate students and professors need to participate in such activities along with school personnel who are also involved as consumers and interpreters of research in a team effort.

"Action research" has been around for a long time. However, as classrooms in the conventional sense change and schools become more open in concept, that research becomes more difficult in some respects. Instead of one teacher and 25 students working together in a self-contained classroom, a school may have three teachers and a variety of aides working with 100 or more students. Researchers not only need different approaches but they also need to work actively on the scene where a variety of teaching and learning methods are occurring.

The challenge, therefore, is to develop closer and more effective relationships between persons who would and can improve schools for everyone and those persons who actually control the schools. Legally, schools in the United States are creatures of the states, not the federal government even though federal programs to improve schools are impressive. Most states, however, delegate responsibilities to local communities and their boards of education. The influences and relationships among the three levels are indeed complex.

Who Shall Speak for Education?

Does one person or any particular group have the right to issue pronouncements on educational change? Persons familiar with the history of American education will recall the many individuals in key positions, specially appointed committees of professional organizations, innumerable external committees and commissions, and other groups that have influenced education significantly.

Several foundations and commissions in recent years have issued statements and recommendations for changing schools. While there is nothing new in this activity, the fact that many different groups are advocating changes indicates that people are reacting to the dissatisfactions ex-

9

pressed overtly by students, parents, teachers, administrators, as well as by persons outside the schools.

The criticisms and proposals to change especially concern secondary schools, although there have been attacks on elementary schools as well. Some specific manifestations of discontent include:

- student activism in the late 1960s;
- the emerging middle school as a protest against the elementary and junior high school programs for children aged 10 to 14;
- criticisms about irrelevant content or wrong emphases in some subjects;
- relatively poor scores on standardized tests of reading, arithmetic, and spelling by minority groups;
- lower scores on tests used for college entrance;
- failure to deliver guidance services effectively to each student;
- inadequate attention to career education;
- increased opposition to higher taxes, caused mainly by rapidly increasing salaries of teachers and administrators.

The concerns are widespread, to be sure.

Many books about education are now in the marketplace. Some offer little help because the authors do not translate their ideas and ideals into practical educational programs that can be understood and accepted by parents, teachers, and taxpayers. Many proposals are ill-conceived, not because of what they say, but because of what they have not said. Individuals and groups often propose simple solutions to complex problems. Whoever speaks for education needs to be specific about what is being proposed as well as about how to implement it. Unfortunately the tendency is for more critical thinking in identifying problems than in developing solutions.

Who shall speak for education? The consensus of as many persons as possible in the local situation is the answer. No knowledgeable person has ever said that improving education is a simple or an easy process. Many persons necessarily need to be involved; the wider the spectrum and the larger the number, the better.

Essential, corollary questions are: To whom shall the proponents of better education speak and how shall they proceed to obtain action? Our times make these questions especially difficult to answer. The legal relationships are well known: state to local boards of education, to central office administrators, to local school administrators, to teachers, and to students. However, increased activities of student and teacher organizations with the tools of strikes and other forms of protests may alter the conventional hierarchial influences. Also, the use of pressure groups, money, prestigious individuals, and the mass media may create other dimensions.

These persons and groups need sound directions and broad perspectives. Specifically they need help in translating their goals, selfish as well as general, into a program that will come closer than what exists today to serving their own interests and the welfare of the total society. Those goals are not as antithetical as many persons today believe.

Chapter 2 provides an overview of a school that is much closer to meeting individual and societal needs than conventional schools do today. Later chapters add more details, further reasons for the changes, plus specifications for developing programs and evaluating the results.

A School for Everyone

Some persons who speak and write publicly seem to believe our society for a number of reasons is headed for catastrophe. This writer is not one of those pessimists.

The Critics Say:
This Is What You Should Do!

IMPROVE READING
SPEND MORE
REDUCE TAXES
HAVE SMALLER CLASSES
LOWER THE TOP COMPULSORY
   ATTENDANCE AGE
HAVE SMALLER SCHOOLS
OPEN THE CAMPUS
EMPHASIZE THE ACADEMICS
SHORTEN SCHOOL HOURS
GET RID OF "ABCDF" GRADES
FOUR DAYS A WEEK INSTEAD OF FIVE
IMPROVE COLLEGE PREPARATION
EMPHASIZE CAREER EDUCATION
MAKE CURRICULUM MORE RELEVANT
   TO YOUTH NEEDS
USE THE COMMUNITY
ASSIGN MORE HOMEWORK
LOOK MORE TO THE FUTURE
REVIVE OLD IDEAS
MORE REQUIRED SUBJECTS
MORE ELECTIVE SUBJECTS
RAISE TEST SCORES
MORE ATHLETICS
ELIMINATE EXTRACURRICU-
   LAR ACTIVITIES
ETC. ETC. ETC.

SCHOOL
EMPLOYEES
BOARD OF
EDUCATION

SCHOOLS OF
EDUCATION
LEGISLATIVE
BODIES

Other persons seem certain that better schools will remedy society's ills. That wishful thinking is attractive. History shows that goal is unrealistic.

But schools can be better than they are—and the teachers and students in them can perform better than they do. The design in this book shows how. Perhaps that improvement in the long run will help society become constructively critical of its institutions—and that is a positive approach to a better world!

Everything in this book has occurred some place and at some time in the United States. It is true literally that so far as schools are concerned there is today nothing new under the sun. The problem is that most schools have not put ideas together in a comprehensive way.

This book presents a rationale and design for a school that aims to make learning so exciting and worthwhile that it becomes a lifetime habit rather than something that is only institutionalized in a school for young people. At the close of each chapter are some possible first steps that can help you and others to progress toward the school for everyone.

Some Possible First Steps
for School Persons

1. Review published statements, locally and elsewhere, for a specific period to analyze what is being said and written about improving schooling and by whom.

2. Prepare a digest, not as recommendations for *immediate* action but as proposals for constructive study and discussions by interested persons who are in a position to initiate helpful actions.

3. Solicit the cooperation and participation of involved persons and groups in your community to conduct a survey (total or sample) to ascertain present local atti-

tudes about education including strengths, weaknesses, and especially constructive ideas for improvement.

For Parents and Others

1. Help school persons to know, understand, and cope constructively with the various individuals and groups who have ideas about school improvement. Recognizing that some have tunnel vision and special hobbies, help to channel their specific interests into concerns about the general welfare. Then take your ideas directly to school persons, rather than merely to write a "letter to the editor" or to some other mass medium.

2. Offer to help school persons in developing better community understandings of the changes that schools need to make.

2

Achieving Personalization

Why is the concept of personalization so fundamental for school improvement? To whom does the concept apply? What positive steps can help each group of school persons to benefit? What are the main components of this design for a school for everyone?

PABLO Casals, the late cellist-conductor, was more than 90 years old when he defined the purpose of education: "We must tell the children, when they are eight or nine, when they can understand the sense of the word: we are a miracle, every one of us. Look at what our hands can do! Tell the children: Beethoven, Michelangelo, Bach, all great people were once children like you. You can be a Michelangelo. You are a unity. This is what parents and teachers must tell children. There never has been and never will be another child like you."

The contributions of any nation to humanity, as well as to itself, relate directly to the degree that each individual reaches maximum potential of self-development and to the extent that each one also has an active interest in and the

15

skills to improve the general welfare. The major concern, therefore, is that each school person—student, teacher, or member of the supervisory-management team—has a program that can help each one to develop his or her own unique characteristics.

There is no conflict between individualization and the general welfare of the total group. Later chapters treat social sensitivity, cooperation, and group needs and goals. In fact, the strength of any group comes from the self-adjustment and vigor of the individuals in it. At the same time, there must be specific programs to develop group concerns that sometimes are ignored when an individual attains personal goals by climbing roughshod over potential competitors.

A *school for everyone* is a concept, a locale, and a program that responds actively to the diagnosed needs of each person.

What does a school look like when personalization is a basic goal? Is it a place where open spaces replace classroom walls? Does each pupil work alone instead of in groups of 25 or 30? Is it a program where teachers seldom interact with students? Are students free to determine what, when, and how they should learn? Are textbooks and other conventional sources of information replaced by learning packages that teachers in the local school prepare or purchase? Does individualization require that students spend more time in the community and less in the school building? Are conventional grade levels abandoned? Are standardized textbooks and competitive examinations eliminated? Do bells no longer ring to separate the school day into standard-length periods?

Two words answer all these questions: "Not necessarily." Some aspects of the ideas expressed in the questions, however, are basic. No wonder that many persons in and out of the profession of teaching, either deliberately or through loose thinking, fail to understand the relationship between individualization and the general welfare.

Personalization in a school is directly proportional to the number of opportunities for choices that the program provides under systematic guidance and supervision.

Concepts such as unrestricted, unstructured, undisciplined, unplanned, deschooled, untaught, and unevaluated are *not* necessarily the ingredients of individualization. Such considerations may be appropriate to some degree for persons who thrive on those arrangements, while others become frustrated and impotent as a result.

Personalized learning and teaching do not automatically require more use of audiovisual devices and less reliance on reading as a learning methodology. Neither does the concept imply a *uniform* reduction of time in school with increased time in the community or at home. The list of alternatives could be extended. The challenge is to develop a program to encourage, serve, and monitor the development and expression of each person's aspirations and talents.

A *school for everyone* must resolve issues and dilemmas in a feasible program better than most schools do now. The design in later chapters shows how to meet the needs within the scope of available financial and other resources. This author has always urged, "Doing better with what you have!"

Individualization for Students

Any school program is personalized to the extent that every student has opportunities with guidance to explore potential interests and talents in all areas of human knowledge and activities. The program described in Chapter 6 reflects the idea that all curricular areas are *equal* in importance. The amount of required learnings in each area is reduced greatly so that each student has time to explore other areas and to go deeply into some of them.

How atrocious it is when conventional schools force pupils in some geographic and cultural areas to spend so much time in remedial reading and mathematics without knowing why and accepting the need at the time! Realistic motivation that stirs pupils in a given environment has to come before remediation has meaning for them.

Teachers, no matter what their speciality, must be responsible for motivating students to study. They must do so continually since interests arise at different times in each student's developmental process. The goal is for every one of them, with allowable variations, to identify personal interests and talents related to the various school subjects and to follow those areas to as great a depth as possible.

For individualization, each student must be able to complete not only the required segments of the curriculum, but also the special interest subjects at a pace that is appropriate for him or her. The conventional idea that all students should complete courses or units of work in the same amount of time is unrealistic. However, personalization does not mean that students work alone. Actually, students work periodically with others who are at the same step of development in a given subject field.

Students learn at home, in communities, and in school. Personalization requires that school programs provide guidance to students in selecting the *best* place to achieve a particular purpose as well as make that place readily available for each of them, as shown in Chapter 7. As is the case in other aspects of individualization, the school program provides information and motivation with respect to these three optional locales and helps each student to choose wisely in terms of personal interests and talents.

Individualization further requires that each student, with guidance, be able to select the most helpful teacher. The school must acquaint students with the talents and interests of all teachers and appropriate non-certificated instructional assistants in the school and with potential instructors in the community. Even though the school has programs designed to help individuals get along better with each other, to deny a student the privilege of learning from someone with whom he or she relates especially well violates the concept of individualization.

Many conventional schools over-emphasize reading and under-emphasize listening, viewing, and doing. One method for all learning is unreasonable. English, foreign languages, mathematics, and social studies all rely heavily on learning by reading. The fine arts, physical education, and practical arts rely more on learning by doing. Science tends to plot a middle ground between the two extremes while also emphasizing laboratory experiences. To claim that any of these methods is superior to the others in all aspects is wrong. Individualization requires that each student uses the methods that are best for him or her as determined with appropriate guidance.

Individualization also requires a variety of carefully planned teaching procedures. Teachers need to motivate students through oral presentations, visual exhibitions, interestingly written materials available for reading, and small-group discussions in which highly motivated students interact with less interested students. Motivation is a process that must occur regularly on a planned basis in all subject areas during every year that students are in school. Chapter 9 tells how to do it.

Another basic feature of individualization is that every student be constantly monitored by a teacher adviser who considers all the data the school has on the student. The adviser helps each one to discover subjects and learning places in which the student has special interests and competencies and then schedules and monitors progress according to procedures described in detail in Chapter 3. Such a program is necessary in all schools. It is absolutely essential in large schools. Counselors with 300 or more students assigned to them cannot effectively provide this assistance to individuals, no matter how hard they try.

Individualization also requires a variety of evaluation procedures to measure each student's progress or the lack of it in all curriculum areas, to record the projects in which each one has had unusual success or difficulty, and to indicate student achievement on measures that provide comparisons with other students on norm-based instruments. However, in harmony with the concept of available options emphasized in this design, the student who prefers a combination type, single-letter grade for evaluation, should receive it.

The point of view expressed here is relevant to all school procedures. For example, if a student wishes to have a teacher assigned by the administration, to be in a conventional class for a standard length of time, or to be involved in other tranditional procedures, the school should provide these arrangements as described in Part 3.

These requirements for individualization and personalization sound like a big order. They are! But the changes can happen in any school—by modifying existing financial and other resources—as shown later in this book.

Personalization for Staffs

The concept of individualization applies also to the teaching staff in much the same way. Individual differences exist among teachers, the differentiated instructional staff, and the supervisory-management team just as they exist among students. Conventional schools, however, establish standard salary schedules, uniform work loads, and other generalized expectations and control over what these individuals should do.

Moreover, the success of these persons often is evaluated on standard instruments applied equally to all of them.

INDIVIDUALIZATION

IS IT?

MOTIVATED
OPTIONALIZED
SOCIALIZED
ADVISED
MONITORED
DIAGNOSED
PRESCRIBED
DIFFERENTIATED
EVALUATED

?

YES!

FOR
EVERYONE

IS IT?

UNSTRUCTURED
UNDISCIPLINED
UNRESTRICTED
UNPLANNED
UNSCHEDULED
UNTAUGHT
UNREAD
UNEVALUATED
UNSCHOOLED

?

NO

21

Members of the supervisory-management team need to help teachers discover and make use of their own interests and talents not only for the students' benefit, but also for personal satisfaction. The concept of differentiated staffing described in Chapter 4 tells how schools organize to fulfill these needs.

Individualization also applies to the members of the supervisory-management team who, like everyone else, possess varied talents and interests. This group includes the school principal, assistant principals, department chairpersons, and others who have special concerns for attendance, discipline, building management, public relations, school finance, community agencies, and the like. They too, need to work in positions and an environment that is most appropriate as described in Chapter 5.

Unfortunately, a "jack-and-jill-of-all-trades" philosophy now applies to the instructional and supervisory staffs. Individualization requires first an analysis of what has to be done, then a determination of who is best able and most interested in performing the various tasks.

Preservice and inservice programs for them, like the students, need to include what everyone has to know and do in order to make the school and the community function as effective learning environments. Then the procedures help each person to find an optimal role in the program, to grow in competence, and be evaluated on the basis of achieving in relation to set goals.

Implications for the School Design

The model to foster personalization among students, teaching staff, and the supervisory-management team must be quite different from usual school patterns that emphasize standard policies for everyone. Later chapters show in detail the differences between uniformity and equality of opportunity in all sizes of schools from the smallest to the largest and in all kinds of locales.

One's initial image of individualization almost always is one of chaos, lack of structure, or of too many people doing what they want to do instead of what the system requires. That image is not correct.

More structure, but of a different kind, is required to develop personalization. However, structures vary with purposes. The design described in great detail throughout this book and synthesized in Chapter 20 is at the same time more complex and more personalized than other schools provide when so much is left to chance.

For example, an on-going argument rages over the question of heterogeneous versus homogeneous grouping of students in schools. The issue typically revolves about whether an individual, regardless of the extent or nature of talents and interests, is better served in a group that is relatively similar in interests or talents, or in a group of diverse characteristics.

Actually, both kinds of groups are essential at different times in terms of the goals to be accomplished. Students of limited talents certainly can learn much from more talented students, provided the evaluation ultimately is not between the two, but rather on the progress that each of them makes as a result of their working together. A talented student may learn much while teaching another student whose present learning is less than his or her own. Of course, highly successful students benefit from working at times with other highly successful ones.

Similar analogies may be drawn with respect to teachers and the supervisory-management team. A school that emphasizes diversity and individualization for adults is a stimulating and helpful place in contrast to the school that develops the same policies and expectations for everyone.

The picture of individualization proposed here is a group of adults trying to help each other, interested in finding what each person does best, looking at tasks to be done, and finding who is most interested in doing particular ones. The whole process assumes that what everyone does is important—and that all tasks in this school are worth doing.

The standards that schools currently follow in defining educational experiences are overly simplistic. Certainly they are not the benchmarks of a society concerned about the welfare of its total population. Today's school policies and practices restrict freedom of choice in many ways. Why should there be a uniform age for entering or leaving school? Is there a single method of teaching that is good for all teachers or all learners? Should a state mandate learning competencies for all students?

Beyond minimum learnings that a school or society determines as essential for all, there are no subjects or any set length of time studying them that constitute defensible requirements for all students. Even the decision about what is essential should be open-ended.

The definition of *teacher*, too, should *not* be limited to include only those who participate in a specified number of years of schooling and take a prescribed set of courses in content and pedagogical methods. Nor should all supervisors and managers have identical training and job expectations.

The school described in this book emphasizes the right to choose and to change minds as added experiences provide a background for better choices. What is right for a person at one time may prove to be wrong at a later time. The program responsibility is to provide the motivation, experience, and opportunity for each individual to make wise decisions.

That too, is a big order! But it can happen if a school is designed to make it so.

24

The Model Unfolds

The model of a *school for everyone,* as detailed in this book, arises from the needs discussed earlier in Chapter 1 and this one. The basic features of the design are indicated here as background for the subsequent explanations.

A triangle represents the three aspects of schooling that help the learners: the people, the program, and the structure. The diagram emphasizes that all three sides of the triangle relate to the learners and also to each other. The details of these components are in subsequent chapters. Further reasons for the changes and how the program operates constitute the material that is essential for decision making relative to the change process in any school.

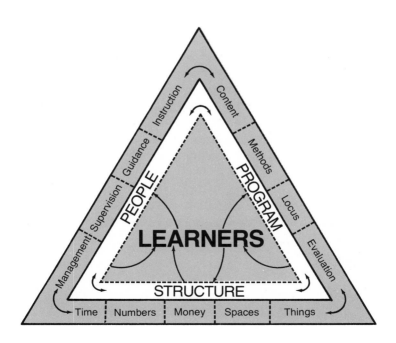

No one knowledgeable about schools has ever said that it is easy to improve the quality of the services they provide. Real difficulties arise in harmonizing professional and lay interests, learner and teacher interests, concerns of the central office of the school district and those of an individual school, and the relationships between a school and such external groups as state departments of education, regional accrediting associations, higher institutions, and employers. Parts 2 and 3 provide specific procedures to follow.

Failure to understand and cope effectively with the interrelatedness of programs in the past has inhibited the potential effectiveness of many school improvements. Changes on any aspect of any side of the triangle affect other aspects and other sides as well. Therefore, careful analyses of changes must be made if they are to be truly productive. How to go about this process is described in considerable detail in Part 4 of this book.

Leadership to harmonize divergent interests and forces comes from a supervisory-management team along with its differentiated staff. This group works with all persons involved and coordinates the comprehensive changes that school improvement requires.

The next chapter focuses on the learners for whom school programs exist. Creating a better environment for them must have priority.

Some Possible First Steps for School Persons

1. Consider the school that you know best and list some aspects for individualization that are most neglected so far as students are concerned. Then indicate which aspects should receive highest priority for study and possible changes.

2. Do the same as in No. 1 but use teachers and/or the supervisory-management team for your investigation.

3. Construct and administer a survey to obtain opinions from the various groups in school and the community about the ideas in this chapter. Tabulate and report the data for use in discussion groups.

For Parents and Others

1. Recall your own schooling and prepare a list of items or ideas about how you as an individual benefited and/or suffered from school policies and practices applied uniformily to everyone.

2. Work cooperatively with school persons to help collect information and constructive opinions from the community to discover common points of view and major agreements on how to personalize education.

People and Involvement

Changes are needed in all aspects of schooling to provide alternatives under proper controls for students, teachers, and supervisor-managers. This design for a school recognizes the individual differences of all persons and utilizies their personal talents to serve them better.

3

Helping Each Student

Is every student in the school known and monitored closely by someone who cares and does not have too many advisees to know? Who is this person, what responsibilities are involved, and what can be done constructively? What do the school counselors do? How do students' needs for individualization relate to their needs for socialization? What programs help to protect individuals and society from persons who violate the rules?

RESENTMENT and uncertainty characterize the mood of many youth today.

A considerable number of these students drop out of schools; some are unemployed and disenchanted by society and its mores. Some are also into drugs and narcotics and involved in petty and even serious crimes. These students and others engage in all sorts of rebellious activities in and out of school; they find fault with curriculum relevance and school policies; and, in general, they are turned off.

Their protests take many forms. Some stay in school because their friends and the action are there. However, their attendance is erratic, behavior poor, achievement low, scores on tests inferior to what they could be, and their boredom is unconcealed.

At the same time, many youth attend school quite regularly and achieve reasonably well. Some, as always, have outstanding productivity as they win awards and please both their parents and school personnel.

School teachers and other officials are frustrated as are their parents when they try to find solutions for disenchanted students and further stimulation for contented ones. It is easy to blame the mass media, government apathy and corruption, the capitalist system, wars, the economy, and other factors over which schools have little control.

The prescriptions to solve the foregoing dilemmas range from lowering the compulsory attendance age to providing early graduation from high school so students may go to college or to work. Both of these solutions and others might be acceptable for some persons. The point is that a *school for everyone* does not apply simple solutions to complex problems, nor does it expect old rules to apply to new games.

Every chapter in this book highlights changes that schools can make to help all students reach higher goals and to cope better with today's societal problems and unrest. What follows here is a specific, positive program to reach student needs faster and more completely.

Personal Attention Is Needed

Imagine a school in which every student, regardless of ability or deportment, is really known and helped by a staff member. It happens when a teacher is personally responsible for monitoring the progress of several students and can take constructive action. Such teacher advisers have basic roles in this book's design for school improvement.

Monitoring means much more than collecting data about progress. The teacher adviser works with each student in the designated group to diagnose problems and analyze successes. Prescriptions are then considered and choices made to help the student.

Implementing a specific prescription may involve changes in program, the place and time for learning, who teaches, the methods used, or other modifications. Thereafter, systematic evaluation produces data for still more diagnoses, possibly some alternative prescriptive actions, implementations, and further evaluations in a continuous effort to discover interests and talents so the student may capitalize on them.

Obviously, a guidance counselor with 300 or more advisees, or an assistant principal or principal with similar numbers, would find such an assignment impossible. A homeroom teacher meeting with 25 to 30 students daily 10 minutes, or 50 minutes once a week, could not fulfill the role either because that time is inadequate and the group-setting interferes with individual conferences. Moreover, homeroom teachers typically cannot change student programs anytime as needed and perform the other services that students require. No wonder that in many schools large numbers of students are neither known nor monitored systematically by anyone. A student has to be very good or very bad to get attention.

Obviously, that system has to change. Accountability for pupil progress in school means much more than keeping track of the subjects completed, grades earned, scores on standardized tests of achievement and ability, and the maintenance of cumulative records.

Schools need systematic arrangements so that every student is known by someone who does not have to consult a file before talking to him or her, or to the parents, a prospective employer, or a college representative about the student's total educational picture. Classroom teachers, it is true, know pupils in their classes, but only as students of their subject. The school, among other things, needs to be a place where every human being is known, systematically cared for, and valued by at least one other person.

Changes for Teachers and Counselors

A teacher has two basic tasks in this school design: one is to teach a school subject; the other is to be a teacher adviser.

In the first role, a teacher is concerned with disseminating an area of human knowledge and with the learner's acquisition of information, concepts, skills, and attitudes. The teacher's relationships with students while they are studying a given subject may be relatively close when they work on a one-to-one basis, or relatively distant when the teacher works with a large group of students—with a variety of situations between the two extremes. But in any situation the focus of interest is basically on one subject field, the one in which the teacher has special expertise.

In the second role the teacher serves as an adviser to a specified number of students. The teacher in this capacity is interested in each student on a wider basis: a human being who is striving to identify and develop special interests and talents. Now there must be unbiased concern about *all* subject fields and the opportunities to learn them in the school, the community, and the home. The student remains in contact with the same teacher adviser for the entire time that the student is in the school unless a change is made for good reasons.

The teacher adviser assumes responsibility for helping 20 to 30 students on a personal basis with their schedules, their independent study programs, their future career and educational interests, and, as a friend, with their everyday problems. The goal is to personalize the education of every student despite varied abilities, interests, and backgrounds.

The school's professionally trained counselors, hence, are free from the routines of program making, checking on attendance, and the kinds of disciplinary problems that often result when students are in the wrong classes, with the wrong teachers, and in the wrong places. Professional counselors have highly specialized training. They should not be expected to participate in the day-by-day instructional process or the diagnostic and prescriptive activities that teacher-advisers use in their work with the students assigned to them.

The Organizational Framework

The basic organizational unit is an advisory group of 300 to 400 students, with one professional counselor and 12 teacher advisers. A school of 1,000 would have three such groups: three counselors and 36 teacher advisers. Larger schools would follow similar ratios. A school with fewer than 300 students has a teacher adviser for each 25 or so students with part-time counselors, e.g., a one-half time counselor and six teacher advisers in a school with about 150 students, sharing counselor services with another school.

Students assigned arbitrarily to a teacher adviser should come from every grade or year in the school so that the teacher will not have to learn a new group of students each year. The assignments are made at random rather than by special interests, abilities, vocational intentions or the like.

Teachers in larger schools are assigned to the advisory groups of 300-400 students so that the teachers in each group are representative of the total staff. Thus a given advisory group includes 12 teachers with a range of years of experience as well as interest in the various subject departments, programs, and projects in the school.

The school principal, and assistant principals in larger schools, are members of the guidance system, each working with one or two clusters of 300-400 students and their teacher advisers and counselors as shown on the chart. Others involved are psychologists, psychometrists, and

Concern and Help For Everyone

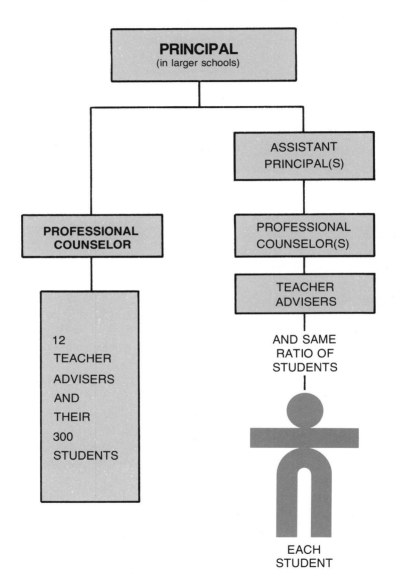

Concern and Help For Everyone

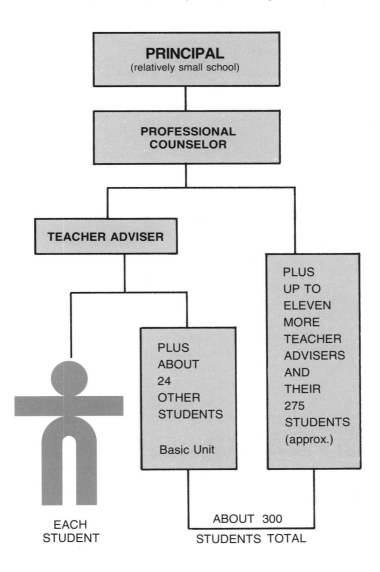

specialists who may be a part of the school staff in a large high school—or in smaller schools as part of the central office staff, available to individual schools on a part-time basis. The chart also shows how the system works in schools of different total enrollments.

This arrangement is not a conventional "house plan" that some schools follow. The purposes here are different because of increased program flexibility and the roles of the teacher advisers.

Such organization assures continued inservice growth of all the professional persons involved as indicated in Chapters 4 and 5. In the early stages of development, teacher advisers should meet regularly, at least once a week, with the counselor. The purpose is to help everyone as they observe the interactions taking place among teacher advisers, students, and counselors. Such meetings are important also for the professional growth of the counselors as they keep in touch with the total school population.

Counselors need to know more about the daily problems that students have both in completing required learnings and in developing their own individual interests and talents. Counselors thereby also learn about the kinds of academic problems that teachers experience. The relationships among professional counseling, therapy advisement, and instructional guidance thus become better understood by everyone.

The expectation is that all teachers in the school will be both advisers and instructors. Of course, some teachers are more effective as teacher advisers while others are better instructors. In spite of these differences, the premise is right. Some teachers may spend more time on curriculum development or other necessary staff functions and for a time not function as advisers. However, if the teacher adviser system is to operate effectively, the entire professional teaching staff, or nearly so, needs to become involved in the program.

The student remains with that same advisory group until leaving the school, unless a change is made by the professional counselor. When transfer from one group to another is desirable, either the student or the teacher adviser initiates the change by petitioning the group counselor. The same approach would occur if a student or a parent does not want to participate at all in the teacher adviser program. If the counselor fails to approve, either party may appeal to the proper assistant principal or principal. Whoever makes the decision does so on the basis of what is best for both the welfare and effectiveness of the persons involved.

A transfer should not be made to discipline a student or to accommodate a student who does not like a decision that has been made by the adviser. Both teachers and students need to learn to participate effectively and responsibly as members of groups. Times arise, of course, when it is better to change membership.

Providing Options for Students

The teacher adviser and the student together develop the individual student's schedule. The data sent from a previous school help to determine where the student fits into the program of continuous learning. How much time the student spends in the various curricular areas and in school, home, or community learning is determined cooperatively by the student and the adviser, ideally with recommendations from parents. The resultant prescriptive action is not permanent because alterations in the student's program and schedule may be made *at any time* when the persons involved believe a change is desirable.

The teacher adviser and the advisory group should meet daily for about 10 minutes, preferably in the morning when announcements are made and attendance is taken. At that time, teacher advisers or students can initiate appointments to get together later in the day.

The frequency of conferences between the teacher adviser and individual advisees varies. Some students need frequent contacts. Others may go for some time without an individual conference. The decision should depend upon need, as felt by either the student or the teacher, rather than by an administrative arrangement that requires conferences at regular intervals.

Teacher advisers know more about their advisees than anyone else in the school. Data of all kinds are channeled to the teacher adviser by others in the school, home, and community. Better communications systems, better techniques for recording and analyzing data, and more clerical assistance for teachers make the program work. Denying teachers these helps would be like asking doctors to serve patients without data, records, and competent assistants.

The school also provides appropriate private—or at least semi-private—offices for advisers for this work and their other tasks as professional teachers. Data processing helps the teacher and advisee to analyze the materials at hand so that together they diagnose and suggest alternative prescriptions to enable the student to move forward.

The teacher adviser has experience and the student has perceptions; together they reach consensus on a tentative action to implement a proper program. Implementation requires determining what is to be learned, where it is to be learned, with whom it is to be learned, and the kinds of data to be collected to measure the degree of outcomes in knowledge, skills, and affective behavior. Both the teacher adviser and student need to know precisely what these goals are in terms that both can understand.

Monitoring students usually requires little time and effort beyond a hurried glance at their reports. At other times and for some students, monitoring requires much effort. The goal, of course, for all students is self-direction and self-evaluation. The kinds of data that need to be gathered and the process of evaluation are discussed in Chapters 13 and 14.

Having a teacher adviser rather than a guidance counselor, assistant principal, or principal responsible for decisions about programs and procedures represents a basic departure in philosophy for most schools. Counselors and administrators working with large numbers of students simply do not have the time to make these kinds of decisions. A *school for everyone* needs to break up the masses of students into smaller groups so that every student is known completely and continuously by someone who has the time and the authority to take constructive action.

The teacher adviser needs to spend an average of about five hours a week on this assignment. If more time is required, the counselor and teacher adviser should analyze whether the teacher is spending time in areas that really belong with the professional counselor. Teachers sometimes become overly involved with their advisees' personal problems in ways that should be handled by counselors.

Group Guidance and Other Arrangements

Some student needs should be handled in group guidance, either in classes or special programs. Counselors and teachers plan and conduct guidance instruction in such matters as bases for selecting programs, pupil personnel services available, elementary psychology, opportunities for advanced education beyond high school, vocational alternatives and employment opportunities, procedures for admission to universities, scholarship information, and other matters of interest to all or many students.

The entire staff should decide where the school will make such information available, what presentations about it are made and by whom, and whom students should see when they have questions relating to these items. Teacher advisers do not have time to provide this information to all of their advisees. Most schools place information in the general library or in the counseling offices. The facilities should include places for printed material as well as areas where students may view and listen to filmstrips and other recorded and visual presentations.

The teacher adviser needs to make sure that students see the appropriate person on the guidance staff in and outside the school. The cluster arrangement shown earlier in this chapter, along with further details in Chapter 5, emphasizes how supervisory-management team members have designated functions to avoid duplication and conflict of interests. Charts and structures make good pictures on paper but, if the school is to help each student to develop maximum potential, the responsibility for that goal has to be placed firmly in one person, that is, the teacher adviser.

The goal is a school in which every student is known by someone who cares and can help to facilitate maximum individual development. No matter how large the school, every student has someone to talk with, someone who does not need to consult a filing system. A parent, an employer, or a college representative now can talk to someone who really knows a student. At the same time, these advisers have back of them skilled persons assigned to help—a professional counselor, a principal, or an assistant principal.

The Individual Student and the Real World

Crime, violence, and vandalism are part of today's society. Daily reports of them fill newspapers, erupt visually on television, noisily on radio, and frequently in the conversations and actions of students. Schools, subject to the same problems, cannot change the societal mores but school programs may help students to become constructively critical of the actions of society, particularly in the locale of the school.

What causes crime, violence, and vandalism *in schools?* There are no simple answers. The student who sees little justice in the system of rewards and punishments (grades, and the like), little relevance in the curriculum, methods of evaluation that stack the cards against him or her, little real concern for personal needs, seeks ways to get attention, withdraws or performs antisocial acts.

The school, like society in general, must take both positive and negative steps to attack the problems. One basic positive step is emphasized in this chapter: the role of the teacher adviser, fully implemented. This development is possible *only* when other program changes are made as outlined in subsequent chapters of this book.

As in society, positive approaches are not likely to achieve complete success, so the school must also utilize law enforcement procedures to the degree necessary. These arrangements include: (a) restrictions in proper relation to infractions of reasonable rules that the group has helped to make; (b) trained officials—not just well-meaning teachers unprepared to cope with criminals—to see that offenders are apprehended and dealt with in order to protect lives and property; and (c) constructive programs to rehabilitate offenders.

These steps will seem harsh for some readers who continue to hope that schools can create a better society. That hope is commendable, worthy of effort, and should never be out of sight. However, until society changes its mores, schools that operate differently face insurmountable obstacles that actually interfere with achieving the humane goals that this school for everyone envisions.

The problem with many schools is that group activities not only are overemphasized but their make-up is determined in advance and continued for at least a semester and more often for a year. Students spend most of their time in *classes*, whose constituency is determined by the particular philosophy that the school follows and by socioeconomic and other external factors that influence enrollments in elective subjects or activities.

The school design in this book includes a number of programs for socialization. Motivational presentations to large groups emphasize equally the importance of all the school subjects. Systematic small groups teach interaction skills through experience and constructive help. Sociometric devices are significant in diagnostic and prescriptive functions. Program evaluation procedures consider all aspects of what the school does and what students, teachers, and supervisors do individually and in groups. Details of all these programs appear later in this book.

The options that the design provides for students give opportunities for those who wish to be in regular classes with one teacher for a specified time to do just that in some subjects or in all of them. The program may require some students to be in groups where movement and conversations are strictly limited. These arrangements result from professional decisions, however, instead of general policies applied to everyone.

The quality of a society depends on the excellence of its individual members and their willingness and ability to cooperate effectively. Individualization and socialization are not opposites. The program plan described here and in subsequent chapters generates quality in both spheres.

Positive Punishments for Doing Wrong

The usual approaches that schools use to deal with students who persist in violating rules involve suspension or expulsion. Some schools even list the number of days that a student will be suspended for committing specified offenses. For example, one school automatically suspends a student for three days when the student is truant for a day— which almost seems like contributing to the offense. Wide variations exist in determining what constitutes causes for expulsion from schools.

A school that seeks to develop the maximum potential of each student must use positive steps to rehabilitate those persons who defy the system. What changes in programs and procedures can help? The school design that unfolds in later chapters of this book has many answers.

The basic approach is diagnosis of individual problems. Why does a student stay at home or go to some other place in the community? Why did the student commit a violent act against another student or a member of the school staff? Equally necessary is the decision on what prescriptive remedy to follow. Alternatives are considered and decisions made to implement one or a combination of them. If the follow-up evaluation is negative, re-diagnosis leads to further prescriptions, and so on.

Most school persons understand the need for the preceding steps but lack of personnel and inadequate programs get in the way of implementation. Some specific steps are recommended in Chapter 11.

This chapter has emphasized the crucial role of the teacher adviser with the supporting help of counselors and other members of the supervisory management team. But positive steps call for many other changes in schools and in the relationships with homes and communities.

These changes are what this book is all about. Chapter 4 shows how teachers in the school find time and different personal assignments to assist the process.

Some Possible First Steps for School Persons

1. Analyze who provides the following services to individual students in your school:

   a. helps decide what courses to take

b. helps decide in which extracurricular activities to participate
c. checks attendance
d. handles discipline, including suspensions and expulsions
e. helps in college or other post-secondary selection
f. analyses grades and other reports of progress
g. analyses standardized test results or other data resulting from inquiry forms and inventories
h. gives advice on health needs or problems
i. gives advice on other personal problems
j. assembles and interprets all information for cumulative records and reports to colleges and employers
k. discusses cumulative record data to help students arrive at prescriptive decisions
l. others

2. Develop cooperatively a transitional plan for improving your school's services to help each student develop personal interests and talents and then systematically seek reactions from all students, staff, parents, and others who would be concerned. Decide which proposals in this chapter need to receive high priority.

For Parents and Others

1. Help the school to plan and conduct surveys to discover what special services to students each group would like to see provided by the school.

4

Teaching as a Profession

What should teachers do? How can they function better? Who can help them improve? How does the system evaluate the productivity and professional growth and satisfactions of teachers? How are individual differences recognized?

MANY groups and individuals have different ideas of what teachers should do. Teacher organizations, individual teachers, boards of education, supervisors, students, parents, and a host of other persons and organizations have revealed frequently and openly how they feel about teaching and how it can be improved.

Many different and sometimes conflicting images of school teachers and their needs emerge. The design presented here aims not only to improve the quality of teaching but to make teaching more professional than it is now.

The need to recognize individual differences among teachers is just as important in school improvement as is recognizing individual differences among learners. Most schools operate as if each teacher is a jack-or-jill-of-all-

47

trades, equally as competent as all other teachers in all fields.

That concept is wrong. Here is why.

Goals of Teacher Organizations

Teacher organizations quite naturally concentrate on higher salaries and improved working conditions as panaceas for improving teaching. The organizations to which most teachers belong, the American Federation of Teachers and the National Education Association, and their local divisions, have similar views on these matters; as a matter of fact, each year they seem to be in closer agreement on what the goals for teachers should be. To attain these goals they engage in strikes, threats, and other techniques successfully used by organized employees in other fields.

For generations, inadequate teachers' salaries in the United States were a national disgrace. The situation is much improved today. The effects of higher salaries are both psychological and real. Teachers need to live in appropriate housing, to dress well, to eat well, and otherwise present an image of professionalism. Higher salaries, as important as they are, however, do not necessarily improve what teachers do in schools. Other factors also need attention.

Teacher organizations also have concerns about working conditions. They urge smaller classes, shorter work days, fewer extraclass activities, appropriate holidays and vacation periods, sick leave, and other welfare provisions. Their signs, protests at board meetings, and other aggressive acts urge these matters even though no evidence exists to show that these factors in isolation produce either better teaching or learning.

They are concerned also about relations with administrators, other teachers, and students. Whether or not these concerns are positive in seeking benefits for others is a matter of opinion rather than demonstrated fact.

Goals That Others Urge

The policies of boards of education, as well as the rules and regulations of school administrators, tend to emphasize the gatekeeping role of teachers. Teachers must be in their rooms at specified times, enforce reasonable discipline, report absenteeism, keep their rooms neat, prepare reports on time, and perform other duties that might be classified mainly as good housekeeping and management.

The emphasis is on process rather than on the product—and that bias is unfortunate. Parents, however, are more concerned about what and how their children learn in school, the grades they receive, the happiness they find, and the respect they develop for their parents and other adults. Parental goals often are limited in scope and vision, and sometimes related to their own social prestige. Some parents actually hope that teachers will not expect too much from them.

Employers judge the value of teaching by the skills which students develop for particular needs, for example, speed and accuracy in typing, precision in keeping records, quality and quantity in performing required tasks, and the like. Others judge teaching by how well teachers respond to their requests to sell items, collect money or other things, participate in contests, or perform tasks related to the purposes of the organization or some aggressive individual.

What students require of teachers is more complex. Some want strict discipline; others want complete freedom. Some want close rapport with teachers while others have less concern in this matter. Some want teachers to be close friends, almost buddies, while others want teachers to be aloof. Some want advisers and advice; some don't. Some seek learning, while others reject it. Students who fail or make low grades use teachers as convenient scapegoats.

Many college professors, on the other hand, urge school teachers to make their students into professional writers, lovers of Elizabethan literature, historians, mathematicians, botanists, physicists, star performers, athletes, mechanics, and so on. The survival of both the professors and universities depends upon the continuing flow of secondary school students to the universities. Their hope is that many of these students will become teachers and go back to the schools to ensure the continued existence of raw materials for them. Their major complaints are when too few students come to them and when the professors have to teach basic skills that school teachers were unable to do.

Not all professors with such questionable motives, however, are in the subject fields; some teach education courses. They, too, sometimes have narrow sights and expect teachers, for example, to be interested more in the social or psychological foundations of education than they are in what occurs in classrooms, even though the two goals are not dichotomous. Some professors of school administration develop fetishes about uniformity, standard policies, and efficiency in management that get in the way of personalization for both students and teachers in schools.

What further complicates the situation is that schools, and therefore teachers, legally are creatures of the 50 states. State legislatures in turn tend to delegate virtually all responsibilities for education to local school boards. Elected or appointed, the board members reflect not only their own ideas but also group pressures about schooling as they establish policies and authorize school budgets.

No wonder so much confusion exists in the minds of teachers and others about what teachers should do and how they should do it. The situation becomes even more complex when one considers the existence of much folklore about teaching and the results from efforts to study the teaching process.

Some Myths To Abandon

Most studies of teaching concern the elementary school level. This situation may tell something about the interests of secondary school educators in studying the process. Nevertheless, considerable research does exist about secondary education. Its quality varies, but the evidence rejects many ideas that are perpetuated by teacher organizations, university professors, school administrators who supervise teachers, and the lay public that develops policies and procedures for schools. We mention a few of these ideas and the evidence for purposes of illustration.

Smaller classes produce better results for learners. Actually, there is little relation between the size of class and student learning as measured by conventional instruments. Small classes often found in wealthy school districts are not the reason for better learning in those districts. Rather, it is home motivation, attitude toward schooling, ownership of materials, and expectations. Environment, not class size, is the reason.

Higher salaries produce better results. Again, the higher salaries paid in suburban areas are not the reason for superior outcomes. Cities that have raised teachers' salaries have found that the quality of teaching and student learning did not automatically improve.

Younger teachers are better than older teachers. Quite to the contrary, some older teachers have learned much on the job and recognize there is much yet to be learned. They are more likely to be innovative and to seek better ways of doing things than recently trained teachers who have not achieved a sense of security. Also, younger teachers are closer to their university days, possibly still heavily influenced by the methods of their academic subject matter professors rather than their education professors who taught them the basic principles of teaching and learning.

The point is that age, sex, subject area, marital status, college attended, and the like, are irrelevant determinants of teaching and learning quality.

Anyone seriously interested in teaching and learning may consult many studies that have been conducted in a variety of schools with diverse teachers and learners. However, it appears that the groups mentioned in the preceding sections are not going to change their attitudes and the pressures they exert by studying research findings.

What can be done to change the foregoing attitudes and misunderstandings? The need is great for teachers to spend more time and use better methods to motivate students, to recognize and provide for individual differences in learning styles and locales, to work with students individually at times and at other times in small groups, to improve evaluation and reward systems, to work on curriculum, and a host of other matters that can make much impact on school improvement.

Most teachers want help and can perform better, provided the system gives them the time and resources that they need. The balance of this chapter and the total school design show how.

Differentiated Staffing and Personalization

Differentiated staffing arose from the need to provide teachers with more time to engage in professional activities, each according to personal talents and interests. At the same time, students would have more adults in the school and community to help in a variety of tasks. This approach to improving instruction replaces the generalized concept that says in effect that there are no individual differences among teachers, that all of them are expected to do everything required of teachers.

Analyses made several times in the past two decades of what teachers were doing in relation to what needed to be done, viewed as a total group, reveal that the school needs per teacher about 20 hours a week of instructional assistants, 10 hours a week of clerical assistants, and five hours a week of services by general aides. In other words, a school with 15 teachers should have per week about 300 hours of services by instructional assistants, 150 hours by clerical assistants, and 75 hours by general aides. Local situations may alter these recommendations slightly; however, considerable experience lends authenticity to them.

Instructional assistants, working side by side with teachers in the various learning centers of the school and in the community, provide a higher ratio of adults to help students than conventional schools provide. In addition to supervising students, the assistants answer questions, prepare materials, evaluate pupil progress in skills and acquiring facts, and perform other tasks as determined by the teachers. Some assistants are former teachers wanting part-time work while others are beginning teachers who have not obtained regular positions. Still others are persons in the community with special skills. All are qualified to help students to complete learning tasks.

Clerical assistants type, duplicate materials, keep records, prepare reports, check routine papers, and do similar tasks that typically now require a third or more of a conventional teacher's time. *General aides* assume many tasks that do not require special competence in specific subject fields. These aides get materials out, put them back, and perform numerous other jobs that have to be done, but not necessarily by teachers or trained clerical workers.

Gains from the System

A differentiated staff helps both teachers and students. Teachers have the time to perform professional tasks that are minimized in conventional schools or not done at all for

"Jack-and-Jill-of-All-Trades"

Monitor
Clerk
Questioner
Supervisor
Servant
Presenter
Adviser
Researcher
Motivator
Discipliner
Writer
Developer
Evaluator
Storer
Repairer
Manager

I Am a
Teacher

I Do
Everything

and so forth!

lack of time. Included are such neglected or inadequately done activities as preparing materials, planning presentations, functioning as teacher advisers, and visiting community areas where students work and learn. The supervisory-management team described in Chapter 5 helps the staff to select activities and to ensure that coordinated services to students are provided.

A second important factor is that, under this arrangement, more adults are in the school to help students and to supervise their progress. Many of these aides relate extremely well to students, even though they may not possess all of the qualifications for a teaching credential.

A third contribution of the concept is it helps teacher organizations and school administrators in the development of an apprenticeship system for beginning teachers. The usual practice has been for a teacher-to-be to go from the status of a university student in the spring to a full-fledged professional in the fall as school opened with the teacher's first fulltime employment. The American Federation of Teachers is not characteristic of labor unions that have negotiated and assisted in the development of apprenticeship programs. The "practice" or "student" teaching that certification requires is an inadequate substitute. The apprenticeship role as a paid instructional assistant helps both the young and experienced teachers in the school.

Perhaps the most significant aspect of differentiated staffing is the contribution of the program to the school's recognition of individual differences among teachers. This arrangement makes it possible for teachers and their assistants to utilize better their own special talents and interests.

The substantial financial and logistical considerations involved with differentiated staffing are presented in Chapter 18. Costs must be related to productivity. A typical teacher now may spend one-third of the time doing work that a secretary could do as well, and possibly better, at a considerably lower salary because of training and general employment conditions. Other factors related to differentiated staffing, including union negotiations, also are discussed in Chapter 18.

Options for Teachers

The *school for everyone* described in this book enables some teachers to spend considerably more time than others in curriculum development, deciding which materials are to be required and which are to be elective as hobbies or careers, a concept discussed elsewhere. Also, as there are self-contained classrooms in this school for students who want and need that setting there are places for teachers who prefer to work alone with students rather than with other teachers.

Some teachers are highly effective in motivating students through large-group presentations. Some enjoy interacting with students in small groups. Some work more effectively than others with students engaged in special projects. Others are most effective in pupil and/or program evaluation, developing workable techniques and instruments as well as creative analyses of the resultant data. Some teachers would spend more time than others in the independent study areas in the school, or in the homes, and the community. The school thus provides a variety of work opportunities for teachers.

The supervisory-management team helps each teacher to find his or her best place in the system. It is important that this team have the proper data about where each teacher performs best. Teachers, through self-diagnosis and aided by members of the team, decide on the prescriptive actions that will increase their job satisfaction and effectiveness.

The supervisory-management team also helps to monitor the success and growth of various staff members as they work cooperatively in a variety of situations. Evaluation of teacher performance thus becomes a cooperative activity that contrasts sharply with what occurs in schools where administrators evaluate teachers with the use of standard checklists or other methods applied uniformly to all of them.

Thus the reward system takes on a dimension beyond merely another step on the salary schedule. Increased job satisfaction comes from having an assignment in harmony with personal talents and interests and from doing it productively for self and for others.

The Teacher Adviser Role Stimulates

The responsibility for helping each student discover and develop personal talents and interests opens the mind of a teacher to the opportunities for learning that the school, home, and community offer. Many persons find much satisfaction in this broader perspective of working with students whose interests and talents differ from their own. It has also acquainted them better with all aspects of the school program as described in Chapter 3.

In the process of using diagnostic and prescriptive procedures with students, a teacher also learns how to use a similar process in finding personal talents and interests. Seeing the opportunities in curriculum fields, other than the ones in which the teacher is a specialist, provides a stimulating experience that may lead to hobbies and interests beyond the subject field that constitutes the teacher's major concern.

Research and Teacher Growth

Schools need to collect more data about teaching not only to help individual teachers become better teachers, but also to suggest research and development programs in schools. Professors and others who have done the research on teaching too often have tunnel vision. They study only a narrow aspect of the activity in an effort to have their findings accepted by other researchers.

For example, in many conventional schools, teachers talk about two-thirds of the time they are in class. That talk is usually unrelated to pupil achievement. A tenth to a sixth of all classroom interaction time is spent asking questions. There is less use of questions in the upper grades than in the lower, however. Interestingly, teachers' use of questions also is unrelated to pupil achievement. Much the same may be said about teachers' giving directions or constructive criticism. Such research findings are interesting and provocative but actually have not produced major changes in teaching styles.

Schools need to collect data systematically on how teachers by departments, rather than as individuals, spend their time, in what activities, in what locations, with what numbers of students, colleagues, parents, other adults, and supervisors, and with what consequences and productivity. Chapter 14 shows how to do it. These data relieve the individual from the concerns of an external, personal evaluation as the department engages in diagnostic efforts to arrive at possible prescriptions for improvement of the total efforts of the group.

As the individual teacher participates in the discussions and actions, there is a better chance for improvement than through the use of the usual rating forms, personal conferences after classroom visits, and other techniques that conventional schools use for that purpose. Since teachers learn the same as students, they need comparable programs. The design for teacher improvement gives them the reasons and the time to improve. Chapter 14 has more details of this program.

This *school for everyone* provides a learning environment for *every* teacher just as it does for *every* student. Since learning is a life-time activity, the school offers more opportunities than periodic university courses or the help that supervisors provide by an occasional visit or consultation. Experiences in universities may enhance motivation and suggest techniques, but genuine improvement occurs in the local school, community, and homes where teachers work with students.

This concept of teachers constantly seeking their own improvement in a school dedicated to the growth of everyone is a basic consideration in the school described in this book.

The methods for improvement outlined here contrast sharply with what goes on in some conventional schools today. That world is a tough one in which teacher grievances against supervisors and managers in the same school are all too common and where the school supervisors join with central office personnel in almost unrelenting conflicts with teachers. That situation is unproductive for both groups and certainly for improving the school program.

How to re-establish communications and joint efforts for mutual improvements is the subject of the next chapter.

Some Possible First Steps
for School Persons

1. Ascertain what teachers as a group do now in the school along with their feelings about the various activities. One approach could involve the use of an activities-setting-outcomes form as described in Chapter 14. Another method could involve a simple inquiry form developed by some members of the staff and then completed by all of them.

2. Organize study and discussion groups to analyze how the school might make better use of the professional competencies of teachers and then make recommendations for improvements.

3. Complete a functional analysis by each department, or those who wish to do so—one that considers organiza-

tional demands and constraints in relation to individual wants or needs present in the faculty.

4. Develop a transitional plan for some of the teachers to implement most, if not all, the recommendations of this chapter for some of the teachers. Be sure the plan is financially feasible for the group of teachers involved by implementing the differentiated staff concepts. Indicate how the results would be evaluated in order to arrive at further prescriptions for improvement.

For Parents and Others

1. Conduct a study to ascertain what representative persons think the total teaching staff is doing now and what ideally they should do—with the goal of understanding better and making positive recommendations about the services.

5
Exerting Positive Leadership

Does the principal have to be a "jack-or-jill-of-all-trades"? Do assistant principals have to be disciplinarians primarily? Who should look after the building, the buses, and the PTA? Does a school need department heads? What other supervisors and managers are essential? Who should prepare all of these persons? Where and how should it be done?

PRINCIPALS have always had problems. They are in the proverbial middle—between the district administration on one side and the students, teachers, and parents in the school on the other side.

Teachers file grievances against them, parents complain to them, students dislike them for unpopular regulations. Supervisors expect them to improve programs and to resolve difficulties.

Years ago a common statement in books and in lectures was "As the principal is, so is the school." People who work in education do indeed know that a major factor in a school's character *is* its principal. Although the principal is

61

certainly not the only responsible person on the staff, forward-looking school programs are usually characterized by competent principals who know how to exert leadership.

Teachers, key persons in a *school for everyone,* learn many methods and develop many skills only after they start teaching. They learn by doing, a change from their college days where mostly they listened to lectures or read books about instructional methodology. Their daily encounters in schools help teachers to develop a readiness for learning about teaching not possible while they were in university preparation programs.

Many teachers today learn their profession through relatively unsystematic ways: by trial and error, informal conversations with colleagues and students, reviewing notes from their university lectures, and sometimes by reading magazines or books. Help may come also from occasional departmental or faculty meetings, or from a supervisor's visit, but all these provisions are relatively uncoordinated and only partly productive.

The school provides teachers an excellent environment for learning how to teach. The principal and other persons involved in supervision and management must help teachers take full advantage of the situation. Thus their students also profit—which is, of course, the ultimate goal.

Three barriers tend to inhibit supervisors and managers in working with teachers. First, the principal is so busy with other activities that the improvement of instruction, which should have top priority, gets pushed aside. Second, the personnel for supervision and management in most schools is inadequate because many people do not understand or accept the importance of effective supervision. This condition leads to the third barrier: many persons now in supervisory and management assignments use ineffective techniques because they do not possess adequate preparation for what they are supposed to do.

The design offered in this book attacks those three problems by changing the number of persons involved and their roles in the process.

Limitations of the Principalship

Most problems of the principalship are rooted in history and expediency. The position originated in the early 1800s when schools outgrew the one-teacher operation and needed one person to be in charge. Parents and others discovered that a committee could not run a school. In time the governing bodies designated one individual as the head or principal teacher.

The early functions of this person involved discipline and record-keeping tasks as well as a full teaching load. The same situation exists today in extremely small schools.

As schools became larger and more management was required, the principal teacher gradually taught fewer classes to have more time for administration. When the tasks became more complex in larger schools, principals hired assistants.

Today's principals are bogged down even more than their predecessors as the job gets larger and larger, mostly with duties and assignments not directly related to improving instruction. One example, recently portrayed in a nationally known newspaper, showed a principal with a stern appearance guarding an empty corridor in a large school—with praise by the newswriter for his police-like duties. There was no mention of the cost-effectiveness of this use of personnel in relation to the need for general program improvement.

Reference was made in the preceding chapter to the increased concerns—and properly so—of teachers for their welfare and resultant increases in salaries and other benefits. Some of the strikes, negotiations, and settlements have had negative influences on the professional relationships between teachers and principals. The natural outcome in some situations has been for principals also to become more militant and concerned about their own welfare. Relationships become strained. In the long run, such developments may bring improvements in schools but only if everyone continues to put major time and efforts on program betterment.

This author produced a film in 1966 to mark the 50th anniversary of the National Association of Secondary School Principals. A portion of the film portrayed the typical principal arriving early at school, greeting the teachers, checking all kinds of building situations, and handling one crisis after another throughout the day. The film shows the principal hours later, at the close of the day, picking up some paper off the floor and turning out the lights after the PTA meeting.

The comment that described the principal's situation was: "Everything that he did had to be done, but did it have to be done *by him?*" At that time, we recommended the supervisory-management team concept. Today's principals have problems, however, that are even more numerous and complex than in 1966.

The addition of personnel only partly solves the difficulties of the principalship. Some persons in the position feel quite comfortable as custodian, public relations expert, director of student activities, chief disciplinarian, negotiator, and master of emergencies. In many cases, the selection of an individual to be principal is based on those skills rather than the person's competence in teaching, in working with others to improve their teaching, or in developing an improved curriculum.

Furthermore, preparation programs for principals in many universities only superficially cover curriculum improvement, teaching methods, learning concepts, and program evaluation. Few persons urge the concept of differentiated staffing for supervision and management, with appropriate selection and preparation, as positive remedial steps.

Despite these problems and practices, many principals are successful in helping teachers and otherwise improving school programs. An encouraging factor in improving education in the past few decades is the increasing awareness by individual teachers and program directors of the key role that principals play in instructional improvement. University preparation programs are providing more experiences and emphases along those lines.

The time is right for extending the concepts of options, differentiated staffing, improved methodology, and better evaluation to the programs of supervision and management. The conventional principalship is changed and the services enhanced in the process.

The Supervisory-Management (S-M) Team

The S-M team in any school includes (identified here by name only since their numbers and functions are described later): principal, assistant principal, building administrator, external relations director, personnel administrator, activities director, and department chairperson.

The S-M team in most secondary schools is understaffed. Also, as is the case with the principal, the services of these persons are not used properly or effectively. Today's assistant principals deal mainly with discipline, school plant and supply management, and extracurricular activities. Guidance counselors work on attendance, discipline, pupil schedules, college admissions, and vocational choices. Department heads spend much of their time on supply and equipment lists and the physical conditions of the facilities they use.

What these S-M members do often has little relation to their preparation. Assistant principals have training similar to principals in management techniques. Guidance counselors are prepared to do case studies and counseling. Department heads may have graduate courses in their subject fields with one or two credits in general school administration.

Here then are the S-M positions and brief outlines of what these persons need to do. The implications are obvious for changes in preparation programs.

The *school principal* is head of the S-M team. This person needs to spend about a quarter of the time supervising, coordinating, and working closely with other members. The principal is liaison between the S-M team in the school and the superintendent and other central office supervisors. The principal also coordinates the relationships of the team with such external groups as universities, state departments of education, and special consultants.

The majority of the principal's time is spent directly on the improvement of instruction. The principal works specifically with all or a selected number of the school departments, depending on the school's size. However, even in the largest schools in major cities and suburbs, the principal spends most of his or her time working directly with teachers on improving instruction.

1. *Assistant Principal(s).* This person, like the principal, has a key role in improving instruction. The number of assistant principals varies with the size of the school. For example, a school with fewer than 500 students would not require an assistant principal with full-time responsibility for instruction, assuming the principal works in this area. For every 1,000 pupils, or major fraction of that number, however, the school needs an assistant principal working full time in cooperation with the principal on instructional improvement. Of course, in the continuum of school sizes, there will be some part-time assistant principals.

2. *Building Administrator.* This individual supervises the general offices, the cafeteria, physical facilities, and trans-

portation systems. Along with the secretarial staff, this staff member sees most visitors and salespersons, sometimes deciding that they need to see other people. With specific training for these assignments and knowing the framework of school objectives, the building administrator makes final and effective decisions.

3. *External Relations Director.* This S-M team member translates the school's financial needs into written proposals to the central office, to all levels of governmental agencies, to foundations, and to other appropriate groups. Financial proposals and the expenditure of moneys translate the school's goals into practice. This person also develops and conducts the school's considerably expanded and improved public relations program.

4. *Personnel Administrator.* This team member supervises attendance, discipline, and guidance. Liaison with other community youth-serving agencies, including police and other juvenile authorities, are part of the assignment. Teachers work with this administrator on their own welfare problems as well as those of their student advisees. Parents and other persons having problems or concerns with school youth see this person.

5. *Activities Director.* This individual develops and oversees student and faculty activities, including the supervision of athletic and non-athletic programs and social events. Community individuals and groups see the activities director in connection with their use of school facilities and other cooperative plans. At times, by local decisions, this person assumes responsibilities assigned to the External Relations Director.

6. *Department Chairpersons.* The number of department heads varies with the size of the school and with the local curriculum philosophy. These persons have major responsibility for curriculum development, including the utilization of the school, community, and home as learning environments. The eight curriculum areas are English, fine

arts, health-fitness-recreation (PE), mathematics, other cultures (foreign language), practical arts, science, and social studies—plus a ninth, religion, in parochial schools.

The departments are combined in smaller schools or in some other schools that are committed to a core or common-learnings philosophy of content organization. How much time a teacher devotes to the role of department head also depends on the size of the school. However, in any school, this role needs positive identification as part of the S-M team.

Notice in the charts that follow how all functions of other S-M team members channel through department chairpersons. This design makes essential more rigorous selection of department heads than is followed in some conventional schools where seniority or rotation systems operate.

The charts that follow show how larger, medium-sized, and smaller schools are organized for proper functioning of the S-M teams. The relationships with the superintendent's office, the community, and with other external agencies are indicated on the chart for larger schools, but they exist for all schools. They are less complex and time-consuming in smaller schools and in smaller communities, but they still constitute problems and challenges with which the S-M team must cope constructively.

Regardless of the size of the school, the principal analyzes the tasks to be done and develops a cooperative group to do them. This function is one of many where university consultants and other experts may provide constructive help, providing their philosophy harmonizes with the indicated needs for improving teaching, learning, and more effective supervision and management of the process.

Program Development

As the single most important person who determines the character of a school, it is essential for the principal to know

S-M TEAM — 2100 STUDENT SCHOOL

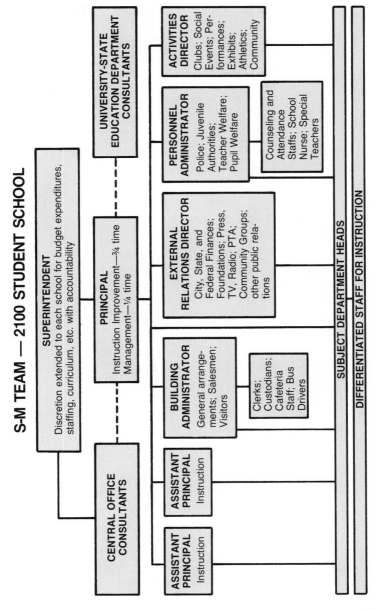

SUPERINTENDENT
Discretion extended to each school for budget expenditures, staffing, curriculum, etc. with accountability

UNIVERSITY-STATE EDUCATION DEPARTMENT CONSULTANTS

PRINCIPAL
Instruction Improvement—¾ time
Management—¼ time

CENTRAL OFFICE CONSULTANTS

ASSISTANT PRINCIPAL
Instruction

ASSISTANT PRINCIPAL
Instruction

BUILDING ADMINISTRATOR
General arrangements; Salesmen; Visitors

Clerks; Custodians; Cafeteria Staff; Bus Drivers

EXTERNAL RELATIONS DIRECTOR
City, State, and Federal Finances; Foundations; Press, TV, Radio; PTA; Community Groups; other public relations

PERSONNEL ADMINISTRATOR
Police; Juvenile Authorities; Teacher Welfare; Pupil Welfare

Counseling and Attendance Staffs; School Nurse; Special Teachers

ACTIVITIES DIRECTOR
Clubs; Social Events; Performances; Exhibits; Athletics; Community

SUBJECT DEPARTMENT HEADS

DIFFERENTIATED STAFF FOR INSTRUCTION

S-M TEAM — 1250 STUDENT SCHOOL

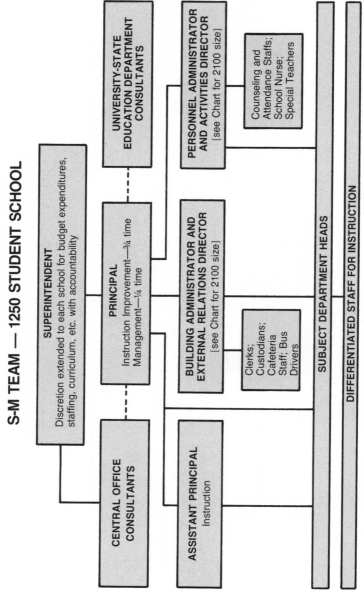

SUPERINTENDENT
Discretion extended to each school for budget expenditures, staffing, curriculum, etc. with accountability

UNIVERSITY-STATE EDUCATION DEPARTMENT CONSULTANTS

CENTRAL OFFICE CONSULTANTS

PRINCIPAL
Instruction Improvement—¾ time
Management—¼ time

ASSISTANT PRINCIPAL
Instruction

BUILDING ADMINISTRATOR AND EXTERNAL RELATIONS DIRECTOR
[see Chart for 2100 size]

Clerks; Custodians; Cafeteria Staff; Bus Drivers

PERSONNEL ADMINISTRATOR AND ACTIVITIES DIRECTOR
[see Chart for 2100 size]

Counseling and Attendance Staffs; School Nurse; Special Teachers

SUBJECT DEPARTMENT HEADS

DIFFERENTIATED STAFF FOR INSTRUCTION

S-M TEAM — 300 STUDENT SCHOOL

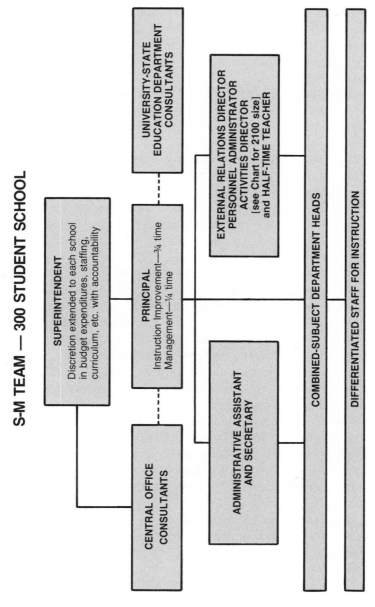

SUPERINTENDENT

Discretion extended to each school in budget expenditures, staffing, curriculum, etc. with accountability

UNIVERSITY-STATE EDUCATION DEPARTMENT CONSULTANTS

CENTRAL OFFICE CONSULTANTS

PRINCIPAL

Instruction Improvement—3/4 time
Management—1/4 time

EXTERNAL RELATIONS DIRECTOR
PERSONNEL ADMINISTRATOR
ACTIVITIES DIRECTOR
[see Chart for 2100 size]
and HALF-TIME TEACHER

ADMINISTRATIVE ASSISTANT AND SECRETARY

COMBINED-SUBJECT DEPARTMENT HEADS

DIFFERENTIATED STAFF FOR INSTRUCTION

and plan the directions of the program. That responsibility requires the principal to read widely, study research reports, listen to teachers and other experts, reflect and cope with the pressures that come from many sources, analyze the many helps that are available, assess the present situation, and develop a sound set of values, ideas, and implemental procedures. Doing these things, the principal will know what needs to happen in the school and will have a program to see that it does.

Most of the principal's efforts are channeled through the S-M team, the group that meets regularly to assess needs, develop programs, and evaluate results. School personnel constantly conduct local studies that provide information about the homes, the community, and the school. The central focus of these studies is on the people and their aspirations and concerns.

The ideas growing out of these studies are presented to the staff, students, and community. The presentations utilize films, other mass media, outside consultants, presentations by individuals or groups already engaged in certain types of activities, or any other appropriate means available to motivate teachers, students, and the community. These presentations are motivational. As such, they should serve as a model, showing all participants how they can use similar techniques.

The motivational presentations are followed by discussion groups in which ideas are clarified, questions raised, efforts carried on to reveal areas of agreement and disagreement, and plans made for implementation and evaluation. Here again, the S-M team demonstrates sound instructional techniques.

The team also facilitates group process. They do not wait for everyone to agree, but concentrate on working with *interested* teachers, students, and community persons. This group is open to new ideas and is willing to try them. At the same time, the door to participation and observation is held open for those students, teachers, parents, and others who prefer to take an option of wait and see or develop still other alternatives. The S-M team makes certain that everyone knows what is going on, although the spotlight is on the inner circle(s) of participants.

The S-M team helps to create a school and community environment that gives new programs a chance to succeed. The environment thus becomes a locale for independent study in which many persons seek to learn new content, procedures, and skills.

When programs are under way, the S-M team frequently visits the places where teaching and learning occur, especially where help is needed. Innovative teachers and students meet frequently to discuss what they are doing and how it is going. Differentiated staff arrangements make time available to do so. The S-M team meets regularly with them, helping to define goals so that participants collect authentic data that measure the results accurately.

There is continuous need to find out how the programs work and how productive they are. Improved methods of program evaluation are discussed in Chapter 14 with emphasis on continuous diagnoses and prescriptions.

Pre-service and Inservice Education

Although staff members in universities work constantly to improve the pre-service preparation programs of principals and other members of the S-M team, the emphasis realistically has to be on inservice growth. Pre-service programs provide background in such subjects as curriculum content and methods of development, social and psychological foundations, methods of evaluation, and techniques for working effectively with people. These pre-service programs are more successful when they include an internship experience so that the prospective S-M team member works in a school while continuing regular contacts with university professors.

The NASSP provided motivation for the development of pre-service internships in a six-year nationwide project.[1] Also organized was a standing Committee of Professors of Secondary School Administration and Supervision that continues to make recommendations for improving pre-service and inservice preparation programs.

Universities have the major responsibility for pre-service preparation with schools making necessary and significant contributions in selecting persons for pre-service preparation, in providing places and local supervision for internships, and in analyzing the needs and successes of their programs. Conversely, continuing inservice education for the S-M team is with the schools where people work with the universities in a variety of support roles. The marriage of school and university personnel is mutually beneficial for both institutions.

Preparation programs must recognize the differentiated functions of S-M team members, and therefore the different content and experiences that the individual needs. No longer should there be unified programs for all secondary school administrators. The major emphasis for principals and assistant principals is on instruction and learning with less attention than now to the tasks assumed by other members of the team.

Building administrators need instruction on office management, food services, physical facilities, supplies and equipment, and the like. *External relations directors* need preparation in school finance and public relations. *Personnel administrators* need comprehensive programs in personnel work with ramifications in schools, homes, and

[1]"A Report on the NASSP Administrative Internship Project," *The Bulletin*, NASSP, Vol. 53, No. 333, January 1969, pp. xi-180.

community. *Activity directors* need preparation in the field of recreation and extracurricular activities in schools, homes, and community. *Department chairpersons* need preparation in curriculum development, teaching methods, evaluation, and the like, as related to their respective areas of specialization.

All members of the S-M team need more and better pre-service and continuing education in the role of the school in society, basic principles of learning, and general understanding of how philosophies of education affect school organization and management. The professors who teach these courses need to spend more time in schools, homes, and community environments to make their instruction immediately relevant to present needs and programs.

The limitations of this book preclude giving the details of pre-service and continuing education programs for the S-M team. Rather, it presents a rationale for a program that is quite different from what universities and schools now provide. The urgency for change in these programs is great. Generalized programs, similar for everyone, have not produced the kinds of persons and services that the times require.

The further education of the S-M team calls for a continuing program. Periodically, members need to attend special institutes, courses, and workshops sponsored by universities, state departments of education, professional associations, and special consultant groups. These programs may last for a weekend, two or three days, or two or three weeks. Moreover, S-M team members need periodically to study full-time to learn the latest research findings, gather innovative ideas, and observe project developments that aim to improve school programs.

Alternatives Add to Quality

The differentiated team provides many options for persons who wish to enter the fields of supervision and management. For example, persons who like public relations and excel at it can find a place on the S-M team without feeling uncomfortable because they are not so well prepared to help in curriculum and teaching methods. Conversely, some may opt for the instructional area, leaving finance, public relations, and activities to others. Also, counselors have a spot for advancement without becoming principals or leaving the school.

Differentiation also facilitates better relations with similarly separated functions in area or central offices of school systems. The same is true in relation to employers, community agencies, state educational departments, and universities.

The image is an S-M team that accepts responsibility for the quality of the total school program. The principal and colleagues place highest priorities on improving teaching and learning. No one outside the school can provide the constant leadership that is needed. Teachers cannot and will not improve instruction solely through negotiations, reading, or participating in conventional inservice activities.

The S-M team is present on the scene. Members demonstrate their influence because they are prepared, concerned, ready for action, and able to perform effectively. The school thus becomes an environment for continuous learning for the total S-M and teaching staff as well as for the students.

Some Possible First Steps for School Persons

1. Ascertain what the principal, assistant principal(s), department heads, and/or other persons involved in supervision and management are doing, the results of their functions, as well as their feelings about the various activities. One approach could involve the use of an activities-setting-outcome form as described in Chapter 14. A related activity would be to keep a log or diary for

selected weeks. Another method would be for the staff to develop a simple inquiry form and then require reports by all of them.

2. Organize study and discussion groups to analyze professional competencies needed by administrators and supervisors and then make recommendations for improving the setting to utilize competencies better.

3. Develop a transitional plan to implement some, if not all, the positions of the supervisory-management team. Analyze what the program would cost. Indicate how the results would be evaluated in order to develop further prescriptions for improvement.

For Parents and Others

1. Conduct a sampling study to determine what representative persons outside the school think supervisory-management team persons are doing now and what ideally they should do—with the goal of understanding better and making positive recommendations about the services.

Program and Structure

Changed views about what the curriculum requires and what is elective provide more relevancy for all students. Systematic use of school, home, and community environments enriches learning and teaching opportunities. Creative approaches to motivation, plus more specific programs to improve human relations, and personalized arrangements for study and work smooth the way for each person. Time, spaces, fiscal expenditures, and school plants are less uniform to serve the diverse needs of everyone. All the foregoing changes help to improve the evaluation of pupil progress as well as the effectiveness of the total program.

6
Making Curriculum Relevant

What determines curricular relevancy? Which curriculum areas are most important and why? How do program offerings cater to the unique interests of every student? Which subjects are career oriented? What are the barriers to curriculum improvement? What are some constructive steps to improve the situation?

A DRAMATIC contrast exists between what many of today's youth want to learn and what schools teach. Television, radio, publications, life in the streets, movies, theater, pornography, as well as libraries, museums, and other cultural offerings plus increased travel have drastically changed the world of youth. These developments should also affect the school curriculum.

The fact is that school requirements remain too much the same. No one knows how many students drop out or do not find satisfaction in school because of inadequate curriculum offerings and restrictive school policies.

When senior high schools by state laws and local regulations require three or four years of English, one or two years of mathematics, two or three years of social studies, one or two years of science, and one to four years of physical education, the students are limited in selecting other courses that may fit better their interests and talents. When the same prescriptions do *not* require the fine and practical arts or linguistic cultures other than English, the program says in effect that those areas are unimportant, or certainly less significant than the others.

Moreover, required courses take up so much time that students have little opportunity to explore possible interests and talents, to make mistakes in curricular selections, and to change their aspirations. Everyone needs to develop hobbies, specialties, and career education interests.

Requiring all students to learn content and develop skills that many of them do not need or want adversely affects the self-image that some students develop during their school years. No one needs such frustration and failure. Rather, everyone needs to find interests and success to the greatest degree possible with improved self-concepts and the positive personal image that those developments produce. A school program needs to emphasize that goal for everyone.

Curriculum Fads and Forces

Although this book emphasizes positive steps to improve schools, occasionally a negative tone is needed to produce a positive thrust for comprehensive change. No aspect of the school program needs this approach more than does the curriculum.

Today's school curriculum is a result of what some aggressive self-styled experts and subject matter specialists have done from time to time to push their subjects to the forefront.

Traditionally, the educator was steeped in the humanities. The study of literature and history, and to some extent the fine arts (but not necessarily the practice of them), were traditional features in secondary education abroad. In the United States, however, a new type of secondary school and curriculum emerged to bring more practical subjects into the curriculum. In a succession of steps, the academy replaced the Latin Grammar School, the high school replaced the academy, and the practical subjects found their way into the curriculum of most schools.

During times of war and national emergencies, the school curriculum emphasized health, physical fitness, and national pride. In the depression years of the 1930s, work-experience education was highlighted. In the 1950s and 1960s, in the interests of national defense and international competition, schools emphasized science, mathematics, and foreign languages.

English and social studies always had high priority in the United States because many citizens were immigrants who needed to be integrated into this culture. The fine arts were relatively unimportant except for talented individuals. Mathematics, science, and foreign languages—emphasized mainly for the gifted and college-bound—were prestigious, and taught in ways to continue that image. The practical arts conversely were emphasized in many instances for low ability and uninterested students, plus those who could not afford to go to college. Physical education stressed competitive sports.

The ninth curricular area, religion, received early support in this country under a colonial act which required outwitting Satan by improving the literacy of the population. In later times, religion was basically a prerogative of Catholic, Lutheran, and Seventh-Day Adventist schools; and, is now prohibited legally in public schools.

The point is that curriculum in the United States has responded to pressure groups and historial influences rather than to careful analyses of what young people really needed. The school has to resolve the dilemma of maintaining existing mores and constructively criticizing them.

Design of Basic Curriculum Needs

The *school for everyone* plays no favorites among the eight areas of human knowledge: English, fine arts, health-fitness-recreation (including physical education), mathematics, other cultures (including their languages), practical arts, science, and social studies (including religion, a separate subject with more and different emphases in parochial schools). No area is more essential than the others.

The foregoing categories represent an arbitrary and conventional classification to which reasonable persons may well object. Obviously, numerous school subjects and general goals cut across the boundaries of the areas. The defense for using them is that they harmonize with society's current expectations, especially in university programs.

Later this chapter urges the need to specify *essential* learnings in the cognitive, skills, and affective domains that all persons should accomplish in each of these subject areas. The point is to reduce drastically the time and efforts that students need to acquire those essential learnings.

A second requirement is to provide opportunities for each student to discover and develop personal *hobbies* and *careers*. Every student needs preparation in the areas that each one selects. Students need not only much more time than now but also special programs to discover their own areas, to explore them in depth, and to arrive at tentative decisions about spare time studies and activities as well as careers.

Essential Learnings

A recent headline in a highly respected newspaper in this country proclaimed "Schools Are Returning to the Three R's." Such headlines arouse interest and are popular because many people have sentimental recollections of earlier days when life was less complicated. Who can recall any school that *ever* abandoned reading, writing, and arith-

BREAK OUT OF THE BOX

HELP EACH PERSON TO FIND PLACES IN HOBBIES AND CAREERS

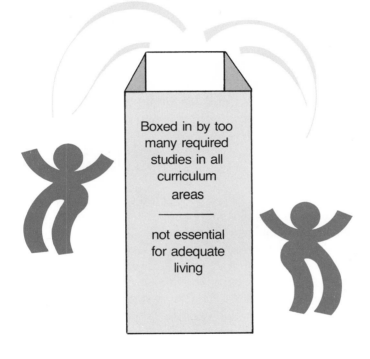

Boxed in by too many required studies in all curriculum areas

not essential for adequate living

REALM OF HOBBIES IN ALL AREAS

WORLD OF CAREERS IN ALL AREAS

metic? Certainly no student can get along in school without these three subjects, nor can any adult live adequately without these essential tools. But other essentials also exist.

Many years ago when communication was much simpler than today, determining what learnings were essential was relatively easy. A Professor Ayres and his students could analyze the handwriting of various occupational groups to determine the quality of handwriting that each required. Accountants had to write very well so others could read their books accurately; housewives needed to read only their own writing!

A Professor Bobbitt and his students could go through the issues of the *Chicago Tribune* and other representative newspapers to determine what mathematics, English, science, and the like, were necessary in order not only to read the newspaper but to understand what was presented there.

Others in the late 1940s conducted similar investigations among parents and different occupational groups to answer the question: what do students need to know in given curricular areas? The results indicated less content and of a different kind than most schools required of all students.

The task of determining *essential* learnings is difficult but certainly not impossible. The biggest problem is that university professors in the various subject fields have little interest in helping to determine curriculum minimum essentials *for everyone.* They prefer to find more persuasive ways to justify their subjects and to engage in propaganda campaigns about their importance for everyone in schools or else limit their interest to specific occupational training.

Other factors involving ethnic as well as economic groups sometimes complicate the picture. Children and youth may see little need for fundamental skills and knowledge. Their parents, however, have learned through sad experience how these shortcomings have limited their employment, social, and economic gains. For example, bilingual education is essential for some, desirable for others, and unnecessary for great numbers; yet schools emphasize foreign languages as important for college admission or cultural reasons.

The determination of what is *essential* must involve persons outside the ranks of professional educators as well as those who work in schools and colleges. Also, such determinations must relate to given places and present needs rather than defined on a state or national basis or for some uncertain need in the future. The point is that a person who has enjoyed learning and profited from it is more likely either as a child or adult to return to a program or to a local school in order to learn some needed geometry, foreign culture, computer program, legal information, consumer skill or what not discovered at a later time.

These situations are cited not to criticize any group but to indicate how reluctant schools are to reduce *required* content so students may have more time to prepare themselves in fields of their choosing and need. Such *selected* learnings relate both to students' advanced university studies and/or to vocational choices, including any further technical training they might undertake. Students thus could enter jobs or universities with more preparation than conventional schools now provide.

Determining what is essential for everyone to know should be initiated by the teachers in a local school. Students in a large city or county may be too varied in backgrounds and needs to have one set of standards applied to all. Certainly, it is out of the question to do so at the state level.

Until schools depart from district or state requirements, the cry of curriculum irrelevancy at the local school will persist and be a vital factor in causing students to drop out of school, both figuratively and literally. Remember, the concern here is only with the *required* content and goals, that which is essential for everyone's survival, and *not* that which may be *desirable* for some individuals and *imperative* for others with specified vocational goals.

Curriculum development in the local school may start with the materials that teachers already possess. Teachers have courses of study or other descriptive materials that indicate what is taught in the primary, middle, junior high, and senior high schools—or whatever those institutions are called in a given locality. These subjects are divided into units, chapters, divisions, or other similar designations. The decision then is to select and use essential materials from those divisions that are related to the learners' needs in a particular subject with reference to the present environment.

Certainly in mathematics all students need to know how to recognize numbers and perform simple computations, to calculate and report taxes, to purchase and utilize materials and services effectively, to develop more precise methods of quantitative thinking, and to achieve other everyday needs that the study of mathematics is supposed to generate.

The next step, also taken at the level of the local school, is for teachers representing *all* of the other departments in the school to analyze and react to the recommendations of the mathematics teachers. Including teachers outside the field of mathematics may help to avoid the kind of general mathematics courses of many years ago that had a little arithmetic, a little algebra, and a little geometry, without reference to student needs.

Students who range from least successful to most successful in mathematics as well as representative parents and employers should also react to the recommendations. The essential curriculum growing out of these studies should be reviewed also by mathematics specialists in the local school system and in neighboring universities.

Curriculum development of essential learnings in all the other curriculum areas should follow the same pattern. For example, in the field of foreign languages—called "other cultures" by some—the goal is not a return to the *general language* movement of the late 1920s and 1930s. The basic purpose includes, but also goes beyond, helping students to understand the origins and other features of their own mother tongue by knowing word derivations and meanings and also achieving appreciation of other cultures. The challenge to the school's teachers of languages other than English is to select content and methods to achieve those goals and to add appreciation of the culture in which these languages operated. The process also calls on the knowledge that students have acquired in social studies and other classes.

Comparable aims are envisioned in all the subject areas. Thus many persons with varied preparations and experience help to develop the school's curriculum of common learnings for everyone.

There need be no concern about a student who moves to a different school with different requirements in common learnings. The special mores of the new environment need to be learned. The program provides the time and motivation to do so.

Pastimes and Careers

An important goal in all curricular areas is to interest students in hobbies or special interests. In foreign language, a hobby might be "tourist" French, Italian, or other language, possibly associated with a charter flight to a country where the language is spoken. The approach would also help students to read, skim simple literature or magazines, and to sing songs in a language other than English. The "pen pals" approach of another era would also be at the hobby level where students want to learn enough language to write simple letters to foreign students or to their own relatives living abroad.

Obviously, a student who has the interest and the talent to go more deeply into another language may find careers open. For example, a student might find employment with a corporation doing extensive business abroad or a position in the foreign service. This type of preparation is as vocational as is specialized training in a machine shop, advanced shorthand, or other examples that could be cited in every curriculum area.

The result is that students and teachers understand and can make selections among the three categories in all the subject areas. First, they know what is required of everyone. Second, they know what provides hobbies for enrichment of leisure time. Third, they know what is essential for career education in the specified area.

Any staff in an elementary or secondary school may initiate productive curriculum development along these lines. That staff naturally will consider what others have done in the same vein, but local conditions always make the curriculum task unique and thus potentially more relevant.

Options in the Curriculum

The school envisioned here presents a completely different approach to curriculum improvement than what occurs in conventional schools. Because of differences among students and locales, national and even statewide solutions to curriculum improvement are both difficult and unwise. Such externally prescribed programs produce many students who are so turned off by their school experiences that in later life they seldom want to read or otherwise pursue knowledge in certain curriculum fields.

The aim here is for school experiences in all subjects to be so pleasant that, in later years, an adult might rediscover a hobby interest in a field not immediately related to the person's chosen career.

The goal is for as many persons as possible to continue to want to learn as long as they live. Too many hours of their time now are spent aimlessly viewing television and motion pictures, randomly reading newspapers, attending lectures, and participating in other relatively passive experiences. Certainly such experiences are not all bad. Some may be motivational and others provide resources for hobbies and careers. More critical selectivity, however, permits the individual to gain time for personal development and social betterment projects that can be more rewarding. School programs certainly can help this process.

The foregoing goal is a long-range one. The immediate aim, as suggested earlier, is to conserve the time and energy of students so they are not worn out completing subjects in which they have little interest or talent. In contrast, they have many more options to help them discover interests, talents, and other experiences that make life more pleasant and productive. Equally important, more of them will make sound career choices.

Curriculum relevance is directly related to the quantity and quality of the alternatives that the school provides. Reducing required content is the first and absolutely essential step toward increasing the curriculum options for students. Equally important is getting away from the so-called elective courses that students had to take for a semester or a year—even when they discovered after a short time that their choice was wrong. The concept urged here is open access and open egress under supervision of the student's teacher adviser.

This discussion of curriculum relevancy deliberately omits emphases on developing creativity, advanced concepts, and other outcomes from higher mental processes. Overemphasis on such desirable goals by curriculum developers and teachers has made schools more difficult and seemingly impractical to many students. Repeatedly we emphasize that a school for everyone provides alternatives. The program challenges the able to exercise their minds to complex thinking and achievements. But the program also provides success without prejudice to other students whose talents and motivations are more limited.

Some schools at various times during the past half-century have introduced core or common learnings programs that cut across subject lines to provide the program of essential learnings and beyond. More recently mini-courses of one to three or four weeks duration or more represent an effort at the hobby level. These efforts and others are options along the trail to better curriculum design. Too often, they become ends in themselves. Wise persons see them as means to curriculum improvement.

The Power and Means

Periodically reference is made to forces that may promote, and sometimes inhibit, change. As mentioned earlier, negative pressures on the curriculum can be exerted by some university professors, parents and community leaders with powerful influences along specialized lines, producers of materials, and some students, teachers, and administrators who have succeeded well under the existing system. They tend to show little sympathy for those persons who have not done so. Some other persons, too, have "axes to grind." No question about it—there are negative forces that work to maintain the status quo or even to return to a past that is sanctified in their minds.

Fortunately, positive forces to improve the curriculum also exist in all of the above groups. Such persons believe that schools could have served them even better and certainly could have helped others more than they did. Their views are altruistic rather than selfish. Beyond those personal feelings, the tremendous explosion of knowledge in all of the subject fields and the more effective distribution of it by the mass media have made teaching and learning easier and more fascinating in this century—and at the same time more complicated.

The plea here is that other powerful groups take more positive and vigorous action to improve curriculum. The reference is specially to the organized teaching profession. The actions of associations and unions during the past decade have produced significant and long overdue gains in salaries and working conditions. Curriculum improvement along the lines suggested in this chapter would be a commendable complementary action. The forces and influence of these teacher organizations could help to offset some of the selfish efforts of other persons and groups.

Much of the thrust for curriculum improvement in the past has come from organizations of principals, supervisors, and other administrative groups. Foundations and industries also have provided funds and exercised influence for school betterment. State departments of education and the U.S. Office of Education provide resources and leadership along with such organized groups as parent-teacher associations, associations of manufacturers and professional groups outside the field of education, organized labor, and others.

The time is ripe for vigorous participation and leadership by organized teacher groups who see improving schools as a professional task and responsibility and who give it as much priority as higher salaries and better working conditions. The goals are not incompatible.

The major barrier to curriculum improvement actually is not the special interest groups. What impedes progress most is lethargy. Students who succeed reasonably well in school see no need to change the present situation. Those who do not succeed protest mildly, only occasionally vociferously, or they leave school. Teachers and administrators alike see no reason to rock the boat when everything is going fairly well. Many parents feel that the school curriculum is not their business. All too often, educators actively or passively promote these feelings.

Curriculum improvement is everyone's business. This school gives all of them better guidelines for doing it. The next chapter adds another dimension by showing where the curriculum occurs.

Some Possible First Steps for School Persons

1. Take a part of any course in the school and indicate what learnings are essential for everyone in the particular school and community in which you work. After that, submit the list to others for their reactions.

2. Make a list of hobbies that are open to a person who knows more and has more skills and appreciations in some aspects of your favorite subject field.

3. Do the same as in No. 1, but list careers.

4. As a student, what are some aspects of your present courses that you would like to study or work for more time if it were available to you? Discuss your responses with a teacher or counselor.

For Parents and Others

1. As an adult, examine part or all of a textbook or course of study that schools now use. What content and suggested learning activities do you regard as essential? Designate what ones are hobby or career-oriented? Communicate your beliefs to the appropriate school department for their consideration.

7
Locations for Learning

What should young people in school learn at home? What should they learn in the community? What must schools teach? How do the answers to these questions relate to what the home, the community, and the school presently provide? How may the answers to those questions influence school programs?

A BOOK about a *school for everyone* has to analyze systematically all places where teaching and learning occur. For example, what do children learn before they enter school? Who are the teachers—in person and on television? What are the methods used, the content, the rewards and punishments, the interpersonal relations, and other conditions?

Children also learn about their neighborhoods and communities long before they go to school. Consider, if you will, the trememdous differences in the settings and the *teachers* in these pre-school experiences!

Entrance into school brings even more complex relationships. Homes yield some functions to schools with varied degrees of willingness and commitment. When the school program fails to serve adequately some children and youth, they either refuse to attend or they become disruptive. Then the school asks the home for help and cooperation. In some cases, the school returns the students to homes and the community by suspension or expulsion! Is that use of the community the best that schools can do?

Learning occurs at all times and in all places, namely in three settings: home, community, and school. Failure to analyze and utilize effectively the unique characteristics of each of these places is one reason education in *schools* is not as effective as it might be. It also limits the potential for learning that *homes* and *communities* provide.

Which of the three is best for specific learning outcomes and how do the three relate? Society can no longer afford to ignore these relationships or fail to understand them. The school described here focuses on this issue constructively.

Important concepts and skills that vitally affect the attitudes of young people, their personal happiness, and their effectiveness as human beings are learned informally at home and in the community from persons who have relatively little formal training in teaching. At the same time many subjects that are less essential for survival are relegated to schools where there are more appropriate instructional settings and teachers with specific training.

Since many youth are turned off by school programs, some people suggest that communities assume more responsibility for providing education away from the school. Communities already have legal responsibilities for providing education as delegated to them by state statutes.

Very few persons, however, suggest that the homes should take over what schools have failed to do. Apparently people believe that the *teachers* in homes—mothers, fathers, brothers, and sisters—have lost their effectiveness as teachers and their ability to create environments favorable for learning.

At the same time people criticize the schools for irrelevant curricula and for the attitudes of their employees who do not relate well to youngsters—especially ghetto and so-called culturally deprived ones and their families.

Enlightened human beings need to analyze systematically *which* locale is best for learning *what*. What should be learned at home and why? What at school and why? What in the community and why? Most of all, how may coordination among the three environments be improved and who should lead in the process?

Highlighting the Issues

The decision-making process can be illustrated by examining an area of learning that is controversial, namely, education about sex. No one can say that learning about sex is unimportant. It certainly should be considered along with learning about the history of our country, how to solve mathematical problems, or how to read and write. Where should learning about sex occur—in the community, in the home, or in the school?

If the school assumes responsibility for sex education, the conventional approach would be for a teacher to make assignments, followed by study and then by a recitation, open discussions, and an examination in a usual classroom with evaluation by an A B C D or F grade! And, of course, remedial classes would soon be organized. No wonder some people object to having the school provide sex education.

If sex education is done in the home, which seems to be the logical place for it, other problems arise. There the *teachers* are the fathers, mothers, brothers, and sisters. In many cases they are incapable or are reluctant to assume the responsibility. Consequently, the home often fails to fulfill the obligation because of neglect and sometimes inadequate information or improper attitudes.

Sex education is generally relegated to the community. The problem is that the community is not well-organized and coordinated to provide the education. The mass media, bookstores, newsstands, theaters, and the like offer materials and programs with relatively undefined standards. Libraries, religious organizations, youth groups, and many others also operate programs, again with minimal coordination or systematic approaches to the youth who need instruction.

The profit motive is significant in what is done. Supervision is minimal. Is this approach the best that an enlightened society can provide? So, students teach each other, many of them with inadequate information and without the proper methodology.

The responsibilities of the school in this area, therefore, become apparent. If sex education is taught in the school with the quality and integrity that the design in this book demands, instruction will be more systematic and better. Therefore, the school is the best place.

Other examples could be cited. Consider the numerous programs and agencies involved in such areas as improving mental health, avoiding drug abuse, preventing crime, and making criminal judgments, just to name a few. Specialists in community agencies, parents, and others in these programs perform many functions that schools also do. They teach reading and other basic skills, develop attitudes toward authority and violators, demonstrate how to improve human relations, and many others. A major need is for improved coordination and planning. The appropriate individuals and groups need to be organized to work together.

The school described here organizes teaching and learning processes differently and also recognizes specific roles for homes and the community. How this division of roles could operate better in sex education and other subjects is indicated by analyzing the responsibilities and methods used in the three settings.

School Responsibilities

Neither simple nor uniform guidelines apply to the three places of learning: school, home, and community. Some homes provide better environments for learning than others; so do some communities. The school staff in co-operation with other agencies needs to determine in each locale how diverse these opportunities are so that enlightened decisions can be made.

One rule-of-thumb is appropriate. The school assumes responsibility for teaching the basics that are *essential* for everyone. Even though some basics may have been learned at home or in the community, the school needs to ascertain whether or not the student has acquired those essential learnings.

The other two aspects of the curriculum as described in the preceding chapter, include the special interests, activities or *hobbies* that enrich the lives of everyone and the *careers* that become available to students who study even more deeply. The school has resources for students who develop special interests and talents but the homes and the community may provide better and more realistic learning experiences.

School teachers organize motivational presentations and discussions that can arouse the interest of all students in learning what the school requires. When community persons as well as family members participate, they add an aura of reality. However, no one else can organize a series of motivational presentations so readily as the school; moreover, the students are there.

The school surveys the community and homes to determine the learning opportunities currently present or that they can develop. Students thus have a catalog of learning resources to use. Finding these resources in the community is relatively easy. It is more difficult to discover systematically the learning opportunities available in homes represented in the school; the differences within and among blocks, neighborhoods, and areas are large. Contacts that teacher advisers have with homes are a great help.

Although the school takes primary responsibility for such inquiries, other organized groups and agencies are involved actively at all stages in the development of the kind of school, community, and home relationships suggested here. The degree to which the school attains active cooperation from others depends on how well those persons understand the program.

The school that uses other resources will see its own expenditures reduced when community agencies and homes systematically assume more responsibilities. For example, when the school no longer assumes responsibility for all instruction related to automobiles, because learning opportunities are provided by garages and other firms, the expenditures for teaching about automobiles in school is less.

Enlisting Community Support

As in developing any new or different program, school persons must prepare carefully. First, they must identify all organized groups that can be brought together for discussions about systematic surveys of the available community opportunities. Service clubs, chambers of commerce, organized labor, civic and patriotic clubs and lodges, women's organizations, church groups, and the like need to participate.

Teachers, school administrators, and members of the board of education represent the school when they explain to other groups why cooperation is needed, what is involved, what gains are anticipated for students as well as for the individuals, the organizations and the community in general, and how the school program would be changed in scope and cost as community agencies assume more responsibility.

STUDY—LEARN—EXPERIENCE

How Much in Each Place?

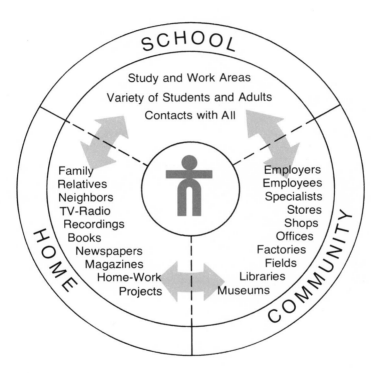

Fortunately, precedents exist to illustrate these efforts. For example, many schools now operate cooperative distributive education programs where students work in various aspects of merchandising and learn good procedures. Students also work in offices, garages, shops, and construction products. They work on boats on the Great Lakes. They study in libraries and in professional offices. The list is extensive; the potential is tremendous. The relationships vary from close, systematic ones to others that are relatively informal.

The school design here organizes these arrangements to benefit both the students and the places where they learn and serve. Also, the school keeps a cumulative record of each student's community learning experiences and outcomes as a part of the dossier described in Chapter 13.

Here are some questions for study in the community. How does government operate in ways that affect people? How may students assist the government? What may be learned at libraries, museums, galleries, religious institutions, private social agencies, and so on? What do offices, factories, and other commercial and service institutions produce? Who does what (labor and management relations), what are the products, and what are the end results (profits and losses), and the like? Students seek answers as visitors, researchers, and/or as part-time employees.

Determining where each student will learn best is a professional decision. It cannot be the same for all students, all communities, or all homes. The conventional school makes only superficial gestures toward the goals described in this chapter. The school that we envision goes far beyond that.

This program planning is quite different from and much more promising than the type of public relations that school systems now conduct. Moreover, the goals are more extensive than the conventional efforts that usually call for increasing taxes to build or remodel, to add new curricula, to increase salaries, and meet other school-centered objectives.

Improved Learning at Home

Teachers and administrators need to understand what learning resources homes can provide. However, teachers and other school officials need not start by taking block-by-block surveys or visiting every home. In many communities, such an activity would be regarded as snooping—beyond the responsibility of teachers and school officials. In some ghetto areas, the visits could be dangerous.

A better way to approach the improvement of school-home relations is through the context of teacher advisers. As the advisers become better acquainted with parental expectations and concerns, they are able to sense responsibilities that parents are willing and able to assume, accepting the individual differences that exist. For example, some "family assistants" and "neighborhood social workers" can provide effective help as paraprofessionals to teacher advisers and guidance counselors.

Consider some aspects of home teaching and learning. What do students learn from newspapers, magazines, television and radio, telephone conversations, and other media? What do students learn from conversations with other youth and with adults at home? What hobby activities and work experiences are occurring at home? What are students learning about such matters as taxation, installment buying, insurance, family budgets, consumer activities, repairing and maintaining household equipment, recreation, care and improvement of house and grounds, and so on? What are they learning in the field of human relations?

Their experiences touch virtually every curriculum area. The school must ascertain to the best possible degree the answers to these questions for every student presently enrolled.

Teachers and others have to keep in mind that the goal is to ascertain what can be learned better at home than in school. *Required learnings* are best taught and learned at *school.* Most standardized "homework assignments" that all students are expected to complete should be done at school. Some homes, on the other hand, may be the best places to learn those things that are unique for each student: special interests, hobbies, and even career education. Some homes may provide very little. Other homes are sophisticated environments for learning and should be used fully.

School teachers and the materials they prepare suggest potential learnings for students at home. Some activities are directly tied into what students are studying at school at a particular time; others are more removed.

How may schools cope with the tremendous differences that the homes present as learning environments? How will what students learn at home be incorporated into their portfolios (record forms) that the school maintains for each student and that teacher advisers use in their diagnostic and prescriptive activities? These questions, with appropriate modifications, illustrate the ones that the school needs to answer with respect to learning at home. There are no uniform data.

Other Potential Effects

When school personnel systematically develop programs to utilize better the home and community as integral parts of the teaching-learning environment, all three may change materially. School personnel will develop wider horizons that include the places where students live, work, and recreate.

Although there are many kinds of teachers in these three environments, the *school* teachers are the true professionals. They have specialized preparation and experience.

They know more than many of the *teachers* in the *homes* and the *community* about how to teach, how to organize learning, and how to evaluate the results. Of course, the school teachers also learn from many of the "teachers" in homes and the community, some of whom have even more formal education than the school persons—or others who have learned in one way or another to become extremely effective instructors.

Thus, the school develops an approach to differentiated staffing that is likely to be more productive than when assistants are brought only into the school. One difference is that most persons in homes and the community are not on the school's payroll. In return, the professional teachers and other employees of the school system provide significant services as they work with the people in the community and homes, adroitly making suggestions from time to time to aid the persons who work with students and report on their activities and progress. At the same time, the various groups of "teachers" can learn from each other.

Providing options to students is the most important part of this design of a *school for everyone*. A student that for one reason or another finds school intolerable does not have to drop out or be suspended or expelled. Nor does the school system have to rent an abandoned warehouse or seek an unused school building to establish a special school that makes better use of the community. Work at home or in the community provides an alternative for students who remain in contact with the school, receiving credit for their accomplishments elsewhere. More is said about these arrangements in Chapter 11.

Building upon Experience

As is the case with many other aspects of this proposed school for *everyone*, the use of alternative learning environments is neither new nor untried. For example, vocational agriculture programs more than a half-century ago effectively combined the three learning environments. Students learned the theory in school and conducted some group experiments there. At the same time, they had individually selected projects that were conducted on the home lot in town or in fields or buildings on a farm. The community provided some materials and even organized fairs to show the products. Students often sold their products in the community with resultant profits or losses. Supervision of the project was done jointly by the school teacher and the parents or guardian, with help from community advisory groups. Such programs were highly productive for many individuals.

Other examples from other curricular areas could be cited. Cooperation of the kind envisioned here for the entire school, for all students, however, is limited in conventional schools mainly to the practical arts, the fine arts, and physical education. Many schools today have an activity called experiential or action learning. Numerous articles and books describe programs where students study and work, with school supervision, in a variety of places away from the school. The *school for everyone* systematically provides programs in all subject areas.

A proposal in one of the major cities of this country is that each secondary school student have one semester of "learning in the community." Both teachers and students would spend a semester in a common learning activity consistent with the general purposes of the school but enriched by using society as a laboratory. The proposed ratio is one teacher with 12 students.

That proposal is cited merely to illustrate thinking along the lines of this book. However, one notices in this example and others the tie-in with conventional school programs in the recommended length of time and staffing ratios. This book urges the abolition of such conventional procedures.

Operational Procedures

The teachers in the school need to work closely together with those in the community. The community experience may be a part of the educational experience of many students but not necessarily for all of them. The amount of time spent in the community and the activities conducted are determined after diagnosis of each individual's needs and possible prescriptive actions that a student and his or her teacher adviser develop with parental consent when legally required. School counselors and other persons of the supervisory management team also help to develop these carefully designed relationships of school, home, and community.

The member of the S-M team, described in Chapter 5, with major responsibility for identifying opportunities for study and work in the community is the *external relations director.* This person works under the general supervision of the school principal with links to the various school departments. The principal or an assistant principal working on instruction coordinates the program.

The school's relations with the individual homes in the community from which students come are conducted by teacher advisers as indicated in Chapter 3. The school's guidance counselors in turn are coordinated by the principal or assistant principal with assistance from the personnel director.

The foregoing programs and personnel illustrate again that a *school for everyone* is not a haphazard operation without controls, adequate supervision, and careful evaluation. Better utilization of all three settings for teaching and learning—school, home, and community—is crucially important in personalizing education.

Chapter 13 describes how evaluation and reporting pupil progress help to monitor the system. The next chapter tells how the school motivates interest in the various locales and, in general, to learn and do more.

Some Possible First Steps
for School Persons

1. Involving all the school departments, analyse homework assignments for a one-week period. After each one, indicate whether the assignment would best a) be done at school b) be done at home c) be done elsewhere in the community d) be done equally well in any of the settings. Summarize and discuss implications of the findings.

2. Survey present *systematic* uses of the community as a learning environment, for example, distributive education, part-time employment, assigned research or papers, participation of students in community musical organizations, etc.

3. Ask each department in the school to take a representative unit or section of some course that the present program offers to students. Analyze what portions could be learned at home or in the community and why it would be appropriate or inappropriate to do it that way.

For Parents and Others

1. As a person in one of these categories, write out your own ideas about how schools, homes, and communities could be utilized better for your personal benefit.

2. Exchange your ideas with other persons like yourself in anticipation of helping school persons to develop better programs along the lines of the presentation in this chapter.

3. Contact the principal of your school to see if you might help to serve the school, possibly as a volunteer.

8

Comprehensive Motivation

What weaknesses in present motivational programs do schools need to overcome? How do systematic presentations help to motivate? What motivates teachers and supervisor-managers? How does motivation relate to evaluation, curriculum development, and where learning occurs?

MANY present approaches to motivation are negative. Schools suspend, even expel students if they do not attend regularly or do not follow existing rules and regulations. School persons notify parents of students' disruptive actions or their failure to measure up to the expectations that the system has determined. Schools also threaten to transfer students to another school or place that is less desirable. Adverse remarks are often placed in their cumulative records or personnel files. There are threats that if an individual does not behave and do well, there will not be a top job, a good college, or better pay.

The conventional school's reward systems presently emphasize higher grades, special awards, better colleges, and enriched jobs. However, personal limitations, poverty conditions, minority group membership, physical handicaps, and other factors often make conventional reward systems difficult or impossible to achieve.

People should understand the consequences of their acts and how these consequences are reported to them and to others. Additional factors, however, need to be considered in motivational programs. Most of the other chapters in this book discuss them. The goal here is to highlight some special procedures, not to disparage all conventional motivational programs. The challenge is to provide optional approaches that work better for a variety of persons and to find which ones are best for given persons.

Motivational Factors for Students

Every aspect of the *school for everyone* has relevance for student motivation. The summary here highlights only a few of the provisions.

Motivational threads must run through the whole process of individualization. For example, motivational materials that introduce a student to learning sequences are usually written; they should also be on tapes, slides, and films since these media are more motivational for many students. Such statements not only show the general content and methodology of what is to be learned, but emphasize the importance of learning it. The appeal is not only to career and hobby interests but also to the enrichment of daily life.

In most conventional schools, where all students start a unit or section of a course at the same time, teachers typically provide some oral, motivational statement. A continuous progress program makes this type of introduction more difficult because students begin units at different times. The solution is to make recorded materials available for individual or group use.

Here are examples of other motivating aspects of this school design:

- The evaluating and reporting system, with available options, aims at positive rather than negative feelings.

- Wider choices in the learning environment—places, selection of teachers, students to work with, varied materials—all contribute to personal interests and potential satisfactions.

- Continuous progress opportunities plus curriculum content that is more relevant to individual needs and interests are conducive to good feelings about the program.

- The teacher adviser is someone who cares and can act on the student's behalf.

This chapter emphasizes a systematic way to stimulate students to go more deeply into a great variety of subjects.

Motivational Presentations to Students

The aim here is to interest students in learning and doing more in a given subject field or activity than the school requires or more than they believe they need or want. The genesis of these presentations was in the "show and tell" programs commonly used in elementary schools and in "assembly programs" that were a part of secondary schools for many years. Not all of these experiences motivated everyone; however, such presentations have provided much stimulation—and still do where they are used.

Outside the school, and in some cases inside, motivation is provided by radio, television, newspapers and magazines, and other forms of mass communication. The idea of "mass" is significant because it implies that the number of persons a school might assemble for these activities may be larger than conventional class size so long as every individual can see and hear.

A major difference between the special motivational presentations that schools organize and the presentations that the mass media use is the degree of specificity for the more specialized needs of the school. However, there are similarities that school programs could utilize to improve motivation.

Motivational presentations need to include a wide variety of topics. Since the basic goal is to interest students in learning more in the various curriculum areas than the students themselves think they want or need to know, as described in Chapter 6, it is extremely important that career and hobby opportunities be used to arouse interest. Each presentation must indicate clearly where the student may go for more information.

Many audiovisual devices typically used in schools have been too stuffy and, like the curriculum, too unrelated to the real world of careers and hobbies where students at all levels of ability have interests. The school envisioned here does not imitate uncritically all practices in broadcasting or commercial motion pictures. On the other hand, by using audiovisual processes better, the school enters a life that is important in the experiences of every student since the day each was born.

This approach also uses printed materials as sources of motivation and enlightenment. Books, magazines, and pamphlets are obvious in the school library and in resource centers of the school and community. Reading at times may be the best motivational experience for students when the levels available are in harmony with the differences among them in interest and ability.

Teacher-pupil planning in connection with motivational presentations is important. Students who have already developed interests may help to excite other students along similar lines. Likewise, students without an interest in anything the school has to offer may provide important suggestions from their out-of-school experiences, ones they not only find interesting but in which they also spend a good deal of time and energy. Certainly the presentations go far beyond the school's conventional awards ceremonies for specially gifted persons.

Faculty members in many schools tend to make most of the presentations. However, the school described here also utilizes regularly three other resources: students, people from the community, and audiovisual devices. There is no rule-of-thumb on how many presentations each should make but the school might well start by dividing them equally. That would mean teachers as a departmental group would prepare nine or ten presentations a year. A similar number would be expected from each of the other three sources.

The program should include weekly presentations in each of the eight or nine major curricular areas as described in Chapter 6. Each of these presentations should last about 30 minutes and be recorded on audio and/or video cassette tapes so they may be repeated if necessary. The school thereby develops a library of such materials for use in independent study activities or by absent students. Also schools may collect presentations developed in other schools or by commercial and university agencies.

The purpose of these motivational presentations requires that all students attend. However, if a student believes that participation in a given curriculum area wastes time, the teacher adviser may remove this experience from that person's schedule. The assumption is that this faculty member knows that the student has made career and hobby decisions, at least for the time being. Therefore, participation is eliminated. Until that decision occurs, all students must attend in order to discover possible interests.

The student audience for these presentations may be relatively large to make better use of the presenter's time.

Although such presentations can be done effectively in large school auditoriums to a thousand and more students, most teachers and others are more comfortable when the groups are much smaller than that number. Typically, the size ranges from 50 to 100 persons.

Teachers sometimes find the task of preparing motivational presentations novel as well as frustrating. Most of them had little training in such motivational techniques. One solution is in the concept of individualization for teachers as indicated in Chapter 4—not all of them need to make the presentations. Some who have talents comparable to what actors possess should carry major responsibilities. Remember, the design calls for only about one-fourth of the presentations to be made by teachers; the others are by carefully selected students, adults outside the school, and audiovisual devices. The variety adds to the motivation.

Motivating School Employees

What the school does for students the program needs to do also for teachers and members of the supervisory-management team. The conventional approach is to provide presentations at local faculty meetings or at state or national conventions. Individual motivation often results from reading bulletins, journals, and other materials, but the outcome is not systematic. The kinds of presentations described earlier in this chapter would replace the conventional faculty meetings that traditionally are concerned with administrative trivia.

Reference was made in Chapter 4 to other changes that the school needs to undertake to motivate teachers. Comparable statements in Chapter 5 applied to the supervisory-management team. Differentiated staffing for both groups requires similar motivational experiences for the various assistants that work with the professional staff.

As a matter of fact, a highly motivated staff may be the single, most important factor in the motivations that students feel. The negative effects of teacher strikes and other evidences of job dissatisfactions may affect student behavior and achievements adversely. The same is true when supervisors and managers have unresolved complaints or unusual problems.

This school for *everyone* seeks many ways to motivate *everyone*.

Putting It All Together

This chapter earlier listed a number of counter-productive motivational efforts which have caused some students, teachers, and administrators to take negative points of view about motivation.

Some extremists urge that the best way to motivate is to give everyone complete freedom in choosing what they want to learn or do, when, and where. The "what-do-you-want-to-do-kids?" syndrome was unfortunate. Some teacher organizations now appear to be taking a similar point of view, that leadership on the part of the supervisory-management team likewise should allow teachers to do whatever they want to do. And the S-M group resents interference from the central office of the school system.

Cooperative planning is a compromise between these two extremes of over-direction and non-direction. Unfortunately, cooperative planning sometimes means that the person in charge—teacher or administrator—sees the task as conning others into doing what the organizer wants them to do. Cooperative planning in fact may be a sham. The school we envision recognizes the problems in these approaches and takes the more positive actions that this book describes in the next chapter.

Students and others need to have choices but they cannot make choices wisely without motivational presentations that stretch their minds and reveal alternative actions available to them. Discussions that follow in small groups help to clarify those alternatives. The curriculum organization and the provisions for study and work make options available. A variety of reward systems and other evaluations also are available in this school for everyone.

An analogous situation relates to teachers and the supervisory-management team. This new school design neither abdicates its responsibilities nor plays games in the motivational process. Systematically developed programs of high quality help to motivate all the persons connected with the school.

Opportunities then exist for persons to pursue the interests they want to develop—with constant suggestions on how to broaden those interests. Personnel policies are developed cooperatively; constant efforts are made to improve conditions for study and work; cooperatively developed systems of rewards exist and genuine interest in working conditions and other matters are present to play a part in the process.

Motivational programs create a format for personal growth through informing, planning, sharing, and developing in contrast to confrontations on such matters as discipline, attendance, extracurricular activities, and other crucial subjects and policies. Motivational presentations stretch minds and set the tone of the school.

Subsequent chapters add other concepts for improved implementations of the ideas thus generated. The next one deals with one important aspect: developing better oral communications skills and human relationships.

Some Possible First Steps for School Persons

1. Prepare cooperatively one or more motivational presentations on some possible alternatives in school improvements for students, teachers, and the supervisory-management group. Avoid as much as possible favoritism for any one proposal.

2. Conduct a study of satisfactions and dissatisfactions that students, teachers, and supervisors-managers feel in the present situation. Have a representative group develop descriptive items on a form or interview that would be answered by "agree-disagree-uncertain" and tabulate the results.

3. Prepare to use the foregoing data in discussions with personnel to arrive at items of greatest dissatisfaction with suggestions of reasonable, constructive approaches and methods of evaluation [see Chapters 10, 11, and 14].

4. Select and implement some action(s) immediately.

5. Be prepared to repeat the process, systematically and continuously.

For Parents and Others

1. Analyze one or more recent programs in a parent-teacher or citizens meeting, or other group that focused on ways to improve the school. Were the presentations constructively motivational? Analyze why or why not for future planning.

9
Improving Human Relations

What must schools do to improve interaction skills and human relations? How does a school teach group participation skills? What kinds of data appraise present situations and suggest improvements?

THIS design teaches interaction skills and human relations in every subject. Conventional schools assign the task mainly to English and social studies teachers in public schools and to religion teachers in parochial schools. These limited programs are inadequate since the need permeates all areas of human concern.

Teachers and supervisors participate in this activity to improve their own as well as the skills of others. Thus the entire school systematically improves communications and human relations. Hopefully, the emphases and methods in schools will have impact also on their communities.

Limitations in Conventional Schools

The typical school class or faculty meeting is too large for effective teaching of discussion, interaction, and human

118

relations skills. Dividing a group into two or three sub-groups in the same setting, however, is not adequate. A teacher with a class of 25 to 30, or a principal with a faculty of 20 or more, cannot be available all the time to assist each small sub-group in their discussions. Moreover, the composition of the groups tends to remain constant, limited by the 25 to 30 students regularly assigned to a conventional class for a semester or year. The situation for the principal and faculty is analogous.

Most students and adults do not know how to conduct discussions either on a one-to-one basis or as a member of a group. Members of the supervisory-management team need to get away from the concept of rule by fiat or authority. So do parent and citizen groups. All groups in fact need to learn not only how to develop and utilize leaders, recorders, and observers, but also the functions served by different types of group members and how all of them relate to each other.

Conventional schools have helped to develop human relations skills on an informal basis but this is inadequate for most people. For example, in some ghetto areas, gang violence has been reduced through conscious use of inter-turf groups, rumor clinics, and weekend training programs in group dynamics. Schools also use remedial groups in human relations. However, everyone needs to learn these skills so that even those individuals less likely to volunteer or those with special problems are included.

Regularly Scheduled Student Groups

The design here provides that *all* students meet in small groups to react to the motivational presentations discussed in Chapter 8. In this *school for everyone*, systematic programs help them to learn the dynamics of groups, interaction skills, and sensitivity to others.

Teaching students to discuss effectively and to respect each other in the process is a new experience for most teachers. Teaching that process is more difficult than teaching how to recite and memorize facts. Moreover, teachers and supervisors themselves, often lacking university preparation in group process, have to study and practice their roles in small group discussions.

So far as students are concerned, the school program has two basic purposes in scheduling these groups. The first is to learn discussion and interaction skills through practice. Originally, the English and social science departments typically had the basic responsibility for teaching these skills. Other departments have an interest in the outcomes but are not likely to be as interested in teaching the basics.

The second purpose is to provide an opportunity for students in all departments to react to and to discuss presentations that they have experienced. The emphasis here is centered more on the presentation, and student reactions to it, than on learning discussion skills; however, teachers are conscious of the benefits that come from proper practice of good techniques.

The *reaction groups* of 15 to 20 students should be scheduled as soon as practicable after the motivational presentations. Fewer students take up too much teacher time; larger numbers reduce the possibilities for individual participation and gain. School persons have learned that 30 minutes is about the right length of time for these group discussions. The number of these meetings each week is determined by the number of presentations. Although the basic purpose is not the development of discussion and interaction skills, these groups permit teachers to appraise how well the school's program teaches these desirable outcomes.

Teachers and counselors determine the make-up of the student groups. However, group composition should be changed frequently. For example, if a teacher determines that two or three students dominate the discussion in a given group, those students should be transferred to another group where there are stronger student discussants so that everyone participates equitably. Both groups, the one that the students were in and the new group, benefit from such a change.

Group composition can have a variety of bases: friendship, emotional maturity, gender, quality of past school work in the subject, special interests, vocational or educational goals, and many others. Counseling records, interest inventories, achievement records, teacher opinions, sociometric, and other appropriate data may be utilized in assigning students to groups or in changing group composition.

Some schools prefer to make the original group assignments on the basis of achievements in the curricular area to produce more homogeneity and better discussions. The fault with that system is that more able students do not have the potential of motivating the less able. No perfect way is apparent.

Developing Group Participation Skills

The first step in developing a program is for the supervisory-management team itself to understand how to organize, conduct, and evaluate group discussions. If no one on the school staff has a background in these processes, an outside consultant probably is needed. The supervisory-management team then teaches the teachers and the teachers instruct the students—so everyone may learn by practice. Most professional libraries have materials that assist persons in learning about improving group processes.

Here is a brief summary of what staff members need to know and do. First of all, there has to be a discussion leader. One issue that divides teachers of small groups is whether a student or a teacher should be selected initially as leader. The arguments pro and con are obvious. If a teacher is incapable or unwilling to relinquish the leadership role, it is probably better that he or she not assume it. However, a teacher-leader for the first two or three meetings can provide a good example of how a leader should relate to the group. Such a brief time permits natural student leadership to emerge.

The first task of any leader, is to help the group decide what to discuss, to clarify issues, and to help the group plan procedures. During the discussion, the leader tries to involve as many persons as possible—for example, noting that some members are not participating, raising the question of what the group is missing by not knowing what those persons are thinking. The leader then may call on some of them for their knowledge or opinions.

If the group departs from the subject of the discussion, the leader tells them what is happening and asks the group to decide whether they want to turn to a new topic or continue discussion of the original one. If the discussion is going badly, the leader calls on the group observer for reactions on why that situation exists. Periodically, the leader calls on the recorder to summarize the discussion to date or asks the consultant for clarification or for more adequate information.

The leader also helps the group to be conscious of the time limits on their meeting and thus helps them to focus their discussion more sharply. All in all, the leader aims to help individual members and the group to become more effective and efficient in their discussions.

Another member of the group has to be appointed recorder. This individual keeps a record of the content of the discussion in order to report to the group on request. Since the group is concerned more with *what* was said than *who* said it, it is unnecessary to record the names of persons making contributions. The recorder notes areas of agreement and disagreement, rather than recording everything that was said by each person. Usually the recorder provides a summary of the discussion at the close of the period, but may be called upon anytime when a report is needed.

A student, in addition to the teacher, is asked to serve as a group observer. This person does not participate regularly in the discussion in order to concentrate on what is happening. The observer usually keeps a tally of individual participations. The teacher may supplement this record by keeping a qualitative appraisal of contributions. Anyone may raise questions on points of evaluation, trying to help the group improve the quality of discussion rather than scolding some people and praising others for what they say.

The teacher, another member of the group, or someone specially invited to meet with the group for a given discussion, serves as a consultant. This person is not expected to give a speech or to monopolize the discussion, but rather to bring specific information and experience that other members of the group may not have. This role is a difficult one for a teacher because of status. The purpose of the consultant is not to set too high a level of discussion or to dominate the group.

On the other hand, if a teacher or other consultant finds a group member making a gross misstatement that misdirects the discussion, the teacher is responsible for correcting that information. Deciding whether the error really matters is a difficult one that tests the consultant's qualities as a helper of students who are learning to discuss more effectively.

Periodically, the teacher meets with the group leader, recorder, and observer to help them grow in their various responsibilities. The teacher also talks to the members of the group, helping them as individuals and as a group to understand better what they are doing. There is need to analyze, for example, the member who contributes little, who talks too much, who gets the group off the subject, who asks irrelevant questions, or who antagonizes. Conversely, positive efforts point out group members who are especially helpful by such actions as introducing desirable information at the right time, summarizing the discussion, clarifying issues, and helping non-cooperative group members become cooperative in the interests of group progress.

Group members must understand what their responsibilities are. Negative roles should be avoided as much as possible—for example, the skeptic who will not listen to the ideas of any other person, the humorist who turns everything into a joke, the pollyanna-type who accepts everything that anyone says without question, or the silent type who keeps personal ideas away from others.

In contrast, there is the creative mind that builds on the ideas of others, the constructive critic who raises questions that will help the group, the deductive and inductive thinker who helps the group to produce sound conclusions, and the person who develops questions and problems for further investigation. The group member who elaborates, harmonizes, summarizes, seeks consensus, and evaluates is an extremely helpful person.

Audio or video tape recordings of small discussion sessions that illustrate good and bad procedures are helpful in judging individual performance as well as total group achievements. Emulating the good roles and avoiding the bad ones are learned through practice and reflection. The English and social studies departments need to provide basic instruction in group processes.

Systematic Program Relationships

These regularly scheduled small-group discussions should occur as soon as possible after the motivational presentations described in Chapter 8. Teachers from the department that arranged the larger-group meetings now meet with small groups of students. While they are doing so, students not involved at this time are supervised in the study and work areas by instructional assistants and a teacher. Remember that these small groups are together for no more than 30 minutes a week in each subject area.

During the large-group presentation, subjects for discussion are suggested. The small group then can request clarification or react to ideas that were highlighted. The teacher meeting with the small group observes what needs to be presented more effectively in future large-group instruction and helps to appraise the most recent one.

Teachers also help to stimulate independent study through small-group discussions by scheduling occasional brief reports from students engaging in special projects. They may also suggest extended study activities that grow out of a discussion or a motivational presentation. Thus the teacher ensures planned relationships among all three of the basic phases of the instructional system.

There are differences between these small groups organized for discussion and the variety of small groups that develop as a part of independent study. Teachers need to instruct some small remedial groups and to help special interest groups. Also, one student teaches another—a group of two—or two or three of them work together. Another group assembles for a reinforcement or remedial session under the direction of a teacher. A study group pursues a goal that has interest or meaning for the participants, for example, a career or a special subject. Such groups are a part of the school's study and work programs.

Evaluating Human Relations

Evaluation here has two dimensions. In the first place, evaluation occurs while the small group is meeting for discussion purposes. Periodically, the teacher or a designated person notes whether a pupil's contribution encouraged further discussion, helped to clarify what was being discussed, facilitated a degree of consensus among the group on the topic under consideration, or was not helpful or actually hindered.

A second type of evaluation comes from the group member serving as observer. This person reports as requested to the group on such matters as the degree to which the group reached the goals of the discussion, how well group members understood what was going on, how wide the participation was, and how well group members respected each other. The summary might describe conclusions or plans of action that developed.

Sociometric techniques also are used to determine the nature of interpersonal relationships with reference to specified goals. To whom would you talk about a specified question or whom would you see to get a stated action underway? What students, teachers, or administrators would you systematically contact for those purposes and others? A series of such investigations reveals who talks to whom and where authority exists.

Sociograms reveal the need for prescriptive programs. Respect for other persons improves as individuals develop wider contacts and understandings of what motivates and satisfies other human beings. This whole area, grossly neglected in most schools, has high priority in the school that this book describes.

The goal of these activities is to develop a climate in which students, teachers, and the supervisory-management team relate better to persons in their own groups as well as across these three groups. The degree to which students and teachers no longer feel in competition with each other, or teachers feel competitiveness with the supervisory-management team, indicates success. People are free to discuss with other human beings not only their personal problems and successes but their proposals for improving the total school program.

Breaking the Barriers

No part of this *school for everyone* is more difficult to achieve than the proper functioning of these small groups. The existing syndrome in schools and the world outside emphasizes one or more persons speaking to a mass audience. The "mass" may be one, a hundred, or millions. Systematic feedback and interaction may be provided but they are seldom immediate and direct.

Nevertheless, some reasonably good examples do exist. Both public service and commercial television occasionally present interaction programs. The press has letters to the editor. Radio has talk-back programs. Civic and special interest groups hold town meetings and comparable programs. Undoubtedly, more would be done if school programs placed more emphasis on the idea.

A school that is more open in concept makes interactions in small groups easier. Teachers come to realize that being in charge of learning no longer requires being front and center, lecturing and asking questions. Supervisor-managers also help to implement the concepts as they reduce the number of total faculty meetings and change the nature of them.

The point is emphasized once more that such small groups are financially feasible within existing budgets. The school can save money as well as staff time by using large groups when appropriate and by increasing the amount and variety of independent study.

The quantity and quality of regularly scheduled discussions in small groups are essential ingredients in reaching the purposes of a school for everyone. Working with small-group discussions challenges high professional competencies on the part of teachers and supervisor-managers. A study of group dynamics helps. Acquaintance with principles of sociometry and behavioral psychology is essential.

Later chapters in this book provide further suggestions on how to start—both for teachers and the S-M team. The next one provides further steps to personalize study and work.

Some Possible First Steps for School Persons

1. Conduct sociometric studies both within and among the three groups in the school—students, teachers, and

supervisor-managers—to produce data on *who talks* to *whom* in order to obtain the given information as listed— or to obtain action on identified concerns. The study should involve everyone; however, the items should be limited to one or two situations to conserve time and energy. Obtain consultant help if needed from the central office or a nearby university.

2. Conduct studies of school climate to indicate degrees of permissiveness, openness, authoritarianism, and so on.

3. Discuss the findings in order to develop constructive remedial programs. Implement the recommendations and repeat the studies to see what changes occur.

4. Analyze group processes in present student, faculty or supervisory meetings as a guide to possible improvements in productivity.

For Parents and Other Persons

1. Recall occasions when you needed information from the school or to talk to some person. What difficulties did you encounter? Who seemed to be most helpful and why? Tabulate your personal answers in order to help school persons understand better the communications problems in your school and community.

2. Apply the principles of group process described in this chapter to your parent meetings or to some other group to which you belong.

10

Personalizing Study and Work

What does independent study really mean? How do conventional school practices differ from and relate to the design in this book? What changes in supervision, facilities, and scheduling are needed to accomplish the purposes? How does the school implement the constraints and privileges of freedom, controls, and independence for each person?

A SCHOOL that stresses independent study recognizes that students have to do the learning and that there is no effective substitute for more personal experiences in school, home, and community. This concept of personal study and work experiences applies to how everyone learns. Teachers, the supervisory-management team, parents, everyone learns basically the same way despite differences in age, experience, and previous training.

This chapter clarifies issues that sometimes confuse, including permissiveness versus control, freedom of choice versus required learnings, individual study versus group learning activities, school study versus learning in homes and community, teacher-dominated versus student-dominated activities, mental versus physical activities, and reading versus listening and viewing.

Independent study encompasses the extremes of these issues and recognizes that what may be appropriate for one learner may not be for another, at one time and not another, nor in a unique locale.

The goal then is to reach all students—from those who come to school only because their friends are there, sometimes to gamble and be more disruptive than attentive, to those honor students at the other extreme who could become even more self-reliant. Comparable extremes, of course with different activities and needs, exist among teachers and supervisors.

Contrasts with Conventional Schools

Most conventional schools structure study for all students in similar places for identical amounts of time and with approximately the same activities and materials. In contrast, this *school for everyone* emphasizes individual differences among students in their talents, interests, and goals. Decisions about study are made individually by each student with a teacher adviser and the teacher in charge of the subject area, with varied amounts of control as needed.

The learning activities—required and elective, school-directed and self-directed, individually-centered and group-centered—constitute independent study, which thus becomes the central function of schooling. The individual's study and work program is supervised by subject matter teachers and the student's teacher adviser who participate in diagnostic, prescriptive, and evaluative activities that help each student fully to develop personal interests and talents.

This concept of independent study requires considerably more structure but of a different nature than that which conventional schools provide. Independent study is not synonymous with terms such as flexible schedules, unstructured time, and open campus. Students are *not* engaged merely in doing what they want to do, when they want to, and where, even though they participate in decision making along those lines.

The amount of time that students in this school for everyone devote to study and work is much greater than most conventional schools provide. Incidentally, conventional schools provide more independent study time in practical arts, fine arts, physical education, and in some aspects of science than in other areas.

Conventional schools also provide relatively more study and work time and better facilities for pupils in kindergarten and first grade than in other years. Children in the kindergarten spend most of their time in independent study; in the first grade they typically spend two-thirds or more of their time in situations where they are not forced to listen to their teacher talk. They engage in such learning activities as reading, filling in blanks, working together, building things, performing, and the like.

The difficulty is that in every school year after the first two or three, most teachers demand more group attention on the part of pupils. This development leaves less time for independent study. Of course, pupils differ in the degree of self-direction, creativity, and performance they can attain, but all can profit from a greater degree of independence than most conventional classrooms provide.

The proposed independent study program recognizes the different interests, talents, and goals that students have. Staff members may suggest, even insist with the consent of the teacher adviser, that a student join a remedial group that meets regularly. Students with special talents and interests also are scheduled for group meetings for indefinite periods of time.

Students in most conventional schools experience a sharp break between full-time school attendance and full-time attendance elsewhere when they complete or terminate their schooling. The school proposed here makes that separation a gradual, carefully planned and supervised experience that occurs over a number of months and years rather than at some dramatic point called "graduation" or "dropping out." Moreover, the school's services continue to be available for persons to drop-in at anytime as needed or desired in what is called lifelong learning.

This school design recognizes that students some day will not be supervised all day long by school teachers and administrators. It strives, therefore, to prepare every student through experience for that time of independence. Every teacher adviser and every subject matter teacher seeks to achieve maximum development of self-reliance and self-direction to assure each student as much success as possible when no longer in regular school attendance.

Options in Supervision

This school for everyone arranges for more adults to help students learn than do conventional schools; moreover, the adults come not only from the school, but also from the community and home. Some community persons that the school selects may not have teaching credentials but all possess competencies for a subject area or activity. Parents and other adults regularly in contact with a student at home receive considerable information from this school so they can know the kind of supervision and help they may be able to provide in their environment.

A variety of persons in the community are recognized officially by the school as instructors in the stores, offices, factories, agencies, museums, or wherever pupils are scheduled for learning activities. It is difficult to over-emphasize the significance of this enlarged and diversified teaching staff for all students.

The school, of course, needs to help students locate potential teachers and locations in the community. In their roles as subject specialists, the teachers in the school develop closer relationships with the practical, employed "teachers" in the community for the potential benefit of everyone. Teacher advisers help students to make selections.

The overall ratio of adults to students, not counting parents, is one to about 12, which provides more adequate supervision with a greater variety of persons available for assistance. This ratio, considerably more favorable to students in this school than in conventional ones, also gives students access to individuals who in many cases bring more relevant and up-to-date supplies and equipment. How all of this program may be accomplished within the range of conventional school expenditures is shown in Chapter 17.

The supervisory-management team sees that these adults in the community understand better than do many conventional school teachers how to provide help when students need it without being overzealous or overly protective, recognizing differences among students' needs for assistance. They provide regular and systematic reports about difficulties and special accomplishments. They strive for the proper balance between over-supervision and under-supervision. The emphasis is on as much freedom of activity and exercise of initiative by students as possible in terms of individual differences among them.

The program encourages students to discover with careful monitoring who can help them most. The open environment enables them to work with one or more other students or to work alone, whichever seems best at the time. Whether the student seeks help most often from the professional teacher in the study center or from some instructional assistant in the school or the community is for the student and teacher adviser to decide.

Some school centers are closely supervised to provide a different learning environment for those students who need or wish more structure. Teacher advisers assign students to a designated room that becomes a home-base for them. The teacher in charge then assumes many functions of the teacher adviser by scheduling each student for agreed on lengths of time to the physical education, fine arts, science, practical arts or other places in the school. Usually the students receive instruction in reading, writing, arithmetic, and other basic subjects in the home-base room. The teacher and assistants establish a non-graded environment somewhat reminiscent of the one-room school but with the advantages of a readily available diversified school and community program.

The teacher in charge of the room keeps close contact with each student's teacher adviser and thus with the home and with community opportunities. The goal, of course, is increased self-direction and control for the students, a purpose that individuals reach at varied degrees and time.

Options in Materials and Facilities

Specially developed materials guide pupils at all age levels and in all curricular areas. Pupils know clearly what the school requires and also what it suggests for additional study and work. The activities include ones of greater depth and ones that stimulate creative efforts. The materials also propose learning possibilities at home and in a variety of community locations.

Required outcomes and optional activities are spelled out in study and work guides (learning activities packages, or whatever title is used) in terms that each pupil can understand. That means that the concepts, skills, and other purposes are defined in behavioral terms to tell each pupil precisely what the school expects. Pretests and post-tests enable students to know when they have attained their goals and are ready to be evaluated officially.

Details about facilities for this school for everyone are in Chapter 12. Just as this school utilizes teacher and student talents and time better, the existing school building has more efficient treatment. Even overcrowded buildings are relieved through better use of space in the school and the community.

The study and work centers that the school provides for each student area are equipped appropriately and decorated, often by students and teachers, to present an image of the particular field. The *study* area is where students read, listen, view, think, write, and converse informally— with frequently used materials readily available to help them cover the required content in the various departments. The library houses materials used by pupils with advanced or unusual projects.

Work areas are where the specialized "tools of the trade" for each subject area are available, for example, science laboratories, gymnasium, woodshop, social studies laboratory, and so on. Because the noise and activity levels vary between the study and work areas, the two are separate although near to each other.

Close to the study and work centers are *conference* areas that provide meeting spaces for relatively small groups of pupils who gather to discuss their study and work projects or to hold meetings with teachers. These rooms have doors and other sound barriers to make them more useful than ordinary open spaces.

Other types of study areas include a few spaces similar to *conventional classrooms*. Pupils who cannot at the moment assume responsibility for their own learning utilize such spaces. Incidentally, their number is smaller than most people realize. As indicated previously, they need close supervision by a teacher whose interest and competence are in helping these pupils to solve their problems, either academic or personal. The goal is to reduce the number of

135

pupils who do their independent study in this intensive care room. While the number of such students will vary from school to school, an average or not more than one or two percent should be in these spaces. If the number grows larger, school persons need to reevaluate the program.

This school also provides a *relaxation* area, a place where pupils go to snack or lunch, talk, watch television, or just sit for a few minutes away from other activities. Like the study areas, it provides a variety of spaces in terms of size and sound control. Unlike the large conventional cafeteria which has to be able to accommodate many adults and students all wanting to eat lunch at about noon, the space may be smaller since not all people are required to eat lunch at the same time.

Adult supervision, as described in Chapter 4, is provided in all of the spaces for independent study and relaxation. Actually, the adults work so cooperatively with students that in most cases their presence is scarcely noticed either by visitors or by the students themselves. On the other hand, the students know the adults are there, ready and willing to help when needed.

The adults recognize their responsibilities to maintain the kind of environment that facilitates the purpose for which the institution exists. The atmosphere is not one of unbridled freedom, disorder, and chaos. To the contrary, it is an appropriate environment for learning, for discussions, for relaxation, and in general for students' personal growth and development. The controls are always there. Disruptive students—fewer in number than in conventional schools— are placed under close supervision with restricted mobility as described earlier.

Options in Scheduling and Attendance

A student's typical schedule includes eight or nine motivational presentations a week, one in each of the major subject areas of the school, each lasting about 30 minutes. Similarly, it includes one small group discussion session in each subject field for the same length of time. Therefore the balance—the work and study time of a student—is 21 to 22 hours, the rest of the week beyond the eight or nine hours that the school requires in large and small groups.

Remember, however, that students do *not* spend this time alone in a secluded space, going through learning packages and passing examinations! There will be regularly scheduled meetings of special interest, remedial, special talented, or other kinds of groups.

The amount of time spent by each student in the various independent areas of the school varies with each person's talents and interests. Both the student and the teacher adviser agree to the time. Thus the 20 to 22 hours per week of independent study time might be divided among three, four, or more subjects and in work or study activities away from the school with conceivably no two student schedules in the school exactly alike. In reality, of course, there is no reason several students cannot have the same schedules if their interests and talents coincide.

The Ultimate Aim

The *school for everyone* sees independent study as the central phase of its efforts. The goal is to develop students who demonstrate personal responsibility for their own learning, intellectual inquiry as revealed by their constant searching for better knowledge, improved skills and satisfactions in achievements, and creativity in seeking new ideas and relationships. The teacher's goal is to become increasingly dispensible as students develop more responsibility for self-direction, self-analysis, and self-correction.

These goals are not achieved in a month or a year—and never completely. However, every student failure along those lines is viewed as a challenge rather than as an excuse to resort to the earlier route of teacher domination and control. Such cop-outs do not improve teaching or learning. Most problems come from inadequate planning and execution—and giving up too easily instead of using further diagnoses and prescriptions.

The school measures its success as an institution by the degree to which the ultimate goal is reached: to teach each person how to be a better independent learner for the rest of his or her life. The school's program and people are basic determinants—so also are how the "things of education" are utilized, as the next chapter proposes.

Some Possible First Steps for School Persons

1. Investigate the present status of study and work in all the school departments in terms of time spent, activities, and location, e.g., supervised in classes, study halls and libraries, homework, and community locales. Are the assignments and activities appropriate?

2. Analyze a series of five consecutive lessons or class sessions in a given subject. How much time does the teacher allow students to think, write, do, and pursue knowledge and skills? How much time do students spend in sitting and waiting for recitations and teacher talk to end?

3. Reduce the number of class meetings per week, e.g., five to four or less, in selected subjects for selected students in order to provide more time for them to engage in independent study under different supervision. Then appraise the results.

4. As a student, how can you learn more in the time you have available? Prepare a proposal to discuss with the appropriate person in your school: counselor, teacher, principal, or whoever is best in your situation.

For Parents and Others

1. As a parent, analyze the present effectiveness of the home as a place for learning. What personal helps can you provide?

2. As an individual or a member of a community group, think through some possible ways that you might help to enrich independent study for the school's students. Then discuss your ideas with school persons.

11

Using Structural Realities

How do people in the school for everyone spend time as they study, teach, or supervise-administer? What numbers are involved? Who selects supplies and equipment? What are the costs? What options are appropriate?

THE *program* and *people* of education should always take precedence over *structure*. Conventional schools tend to reverse that order. Some of the controversies, strikes, and governing board policies—as well as existing criteria for judging school excellence—often make the same mistake. Structure serves people and program.

The school's structural realities include the elements of time, numbers, spaces, supplies and equipment, and money. How students, teachers, and the supervisory-management team use these elements to improve teaching and learning—and utlimately the quality of what occurs in the school, community, and homes—must be analyzed frequently. Using the structural realities differently assures a unique educational setting.

Since changes in the *things* of education produce few threats to people and programs, the tendency in conventional schools is to focus on these elements to produce a favorable image. However, a new building with modern supplies and equipment may have little bearing on what teachers and learners do. A flexible schedule that provides 30- or 20-minute modules of time (instead of the usual 50-minute class periods), with most classes meeting for two or three "mods," may not in fact change the way that students and teachers utilize their time. Many other examples are easily cited.

Spending increased sums of money on teachers' salaries enables teachers to enjoy higher standards of living but does not necessarily improve the quality of teaching or learning. Neither does increasing the number of persons employed in central or regional offices to administer and supervise schools automatically improve a school's program. We do not argue against these developments, but we must emphasize that by themselves such changes do not improve schools. How the structural elements are utilized, however, is crucial.

The Element of Time

How time is used determines the character of institutions and people. A student who passively listens to teachers talk and to other students' answers, especially *wrong* answers, does not use time productively. A school system that schedules standard length class periods and controls the time by sounding bells every 30 or 60 minutes does not help students learn how to use time productively.

How a school uses time has financial as well as programatic implications. Studies indicate that teachers talk to students about two-thirds of the time that school is in session, an activity that is relatively unproductive for most students and teachers. Changing the way students and teachers spend time merely by adopting some form of flexible scheduling to vary class periods does not have much value, however, unless basic changes in methods and programs are implemented.

One way to change the use of time is to reduce drastically the amount of teacher talk in front of organized groups of students that are captive audiences. The corollary is to increase, in an equally dramatic manner, the amount of time that students devote to various study and work activities in schools, home, and communities. Teachers also benefit because they have time for other potentially more productive activities.

The school described here has no uniform prescriptions for the use of time for students, teachers, and supervisor-managers. The student and teacher adviser together decide how the student spends time. The supervisor and teacher together decide how the teacher spends time. Supervisor-managers in cooperation with their colleagues in the school and in the central office decide how each of the S-M group spends time. Of course, the system needs to make some decisions on the uses of time that apply to everyone: for example, when meals or snacks are served, when presentations and reaction groups are scheduled, when buses operate, and when the school building opens and closes.

The amount of time that the system allows for completing tasks must recognize individual differences. The amount of credit that a student receives for completing an assignment or a course should not be based on the amount of time spent in completing it. The program may provide suggestions on typical or average lengths of time but should not subject persons to arbitrary controls that ignore individual differences in motivation, skills, and interests.

This concept does not imply that the school does not know where students or teachers are at given times. Having made a decision with the advice and consent of his or her adviser, a student is obligated to allocate time accordingly.

The important difference between this program and the conventional school is that these decisions are student centered, under personal supervision, rather than institutionally centered with uniform requirements for everyone. An analogous situation applies to teachers and supervisor-managers.

Available space in the school or in the community may restrict the use of time. However, such restrictions should be considered temporary, with the goal to change time as soon as it is possible to do so. Thus, the school design here helps every individual to plan more productive use of time than the conventional school program allows. For example, research has produced sound evidence that motivated students who need and spend more time than others on basic skills instruction have significant improvement in learning outcomes.

The use of time is supervised by human beings rather than by a program clock. Careful planning avoids the chaos that brought the bell system in the first place. The school has clocks and individuals have watches. Preparation for life requires experiences in using effectively these devices and the hours they designate. As a reminder, a relatively quiet buzzer may designate hours and half-hours.

The Use of Numbers

What is said about the use of time is applicable to the use of numbers. As far as students are concerned, the school has many kinds of groups ranging in size from one to many students. The size of each group depends on its purposes.

When increased use of independent study was emphasized by this writer and others several years ago, the first reaction in schools was to provide individual study carrels to allow each student a private niche with visual separation from other persons; the group size was *one* person. Some students need this kind of setting, but not all of them; in fact, most students prefer to study with other students in various sized groups. More often than not, students work in pairs, although in many cases the group is three, four, five, or even more working together.

How many is determined by student interests, habits, and the task that is undertaken. There cannot be, nor should there be, any rule of thumb to govern the numbers in these activities. It is just as wrong in a laboratory to insist that every student should have a partner as it is to expect every student to work alone.

Students spend 80 percent or more of their time in activities that are not scheduled for a semester or a year as regular "classes." However, this does not mean that they spend that much time alone or in groups of two or three, or any other specified number.

The number of students that are assembled for a given task, remedial or special interest, varies with the needs and the purposes of the students. This school design presents various teaching and learning activities with different numbers in groups, depending upon purposes and needs rather than a predetermined size. A remedial group may have one or two persons, or a dozen or more who need a particular kind of activity. A special interest group of a given size may meet for an extended period of time so that students can learn together, exchange ideas, display products, take field trips, or engage in a variety of other activities. Of course, an official basketball team has five players at one time in a game; there are some rigid group sizes.

When the pedagogical purpose is to introduce a group to ideas or to motivate students who may engage in the activity, the size of the group is irrelevant so long as each person can see and hear well. The purposes, the method of presentation, the effectiveness of the presentor, and the interest of the subject are factors that influence size.

Following such a motivational presentation, the students are assembled in small groups for reactions and questions.

144

The aim is to develop skills of discussion and interaction. As indicated in Chapter 9, the optimum number for these groups is approximately 15. If the number is much larger, individuals find it difficult to participate and raise questions in the time that the group meets. If the groups are smaller, it takes too many teachers and too much time to meet with the groups in relation to other priorities.

Spaces, Supplies, and Equipment

The school design here departs often from standardized numbers and policies. Just as it has no standard class size or teacher-pupil ratio, there are no uniform sizes for classrooms, numbers of library books, lists of supplies and equipment in relation to the number of students, and the like. Rather, a variety of spaces are determined by purpose and use. Moreover, the program no longer insists that all learning takes place in a school building. The community and home also provide useful learning environments.

Standard lists of supplies and equipment imposed by central business and purchasing offices are an educational curse as well as a waste of money. The responsibility of these offices should be to hear salespersons and assemble information that teachers and administrators can use in determining which supplies and equipment are most useful and practical, as well as financially feasible, for the needs of their school program.

The central office alerts school groups to ideas, samples, descriptive materials, and the like, so that persons in the local schools have the necessary information to make wise choices. Central office personnel also may devise instruments that help school people evaluate the relative productivity of these materials.

Local school staffs decide about supplies and equipment with help from the school's supervisory-management team. Individual teachers are forced to learn about materials. They

145

also are prevented from making unwise decisions in spending the usually inadequate funds available for these purposes or from unnecessary duplications of what others may order. Business administrators in local and central school offices then use sound procedures in purchasing, ordering, and delivering the materials. However, they are not obsessed with huge quantity purchases which are thrust upon everyone and sometimes not used.

The Use of Money

The "doing better with what you have" philosophy of the school that this book envisions requires that the amount of money available for operating conventional schools also be available to the school where the program is more individualized. The school should aim to spend neither more nor less than conventional schools. The relationships between money and productivity or consequences need to be understood and measured systematically. How money is spent determines the character of institutions and people.

This author for many years advocated higher salaries for teachers and other school employees. Teachers should be able to live like other professional persons and successful workers. There is no reason that teachers' satisfactions from their work should be their main reward, rather than money. We do not apply such a standard to business people, farmers, or other workers.

On the other hand, teacher organizations' pleas for higher salaries on the basis of improved productivity and better learning results by students are unsupportable. Higher salaries enable teachers to live better but do not automatically improve teaching quality. Job satisfaction and morale are influenced by higher salaries, which could conceivably cause better teaching, but certainly this is not always the case.

The purpose of a school is to serve the interests of students. However, the school also provides a pleasant and profitable place for teachers and the supervisory-management team to work and to earn a living. Earning a good living is extremely important in business and in other human endeavors and for the same reasons should be accepted as important in schools.

The construction of a school as a monument to the community, one which the chamber of commerce and citizens point to with pride, may be a defensible reason for expending large sums of money, but it certainly does not automatically increase the quality of teaching and learning. To live in comfortable and inspirational surroundings is pleasant, but an old building with proper levels of comfort and beauty may also be a satisfactory environment. An old school building may not provide the community pride that comes from the external appearance of a new structure, but the expenditure of money on the edifice itself needs to be considered carefully in relation to other needs.

Similar principles apply to all aspects of the school as described in other chapters of this book. The needs of differentiated staffing, diverse kinds of supplies and equipment, the varied grouping of students for teaching and learning, and all the rest, have implications for the manner in which school moneys are spent.

Standard formulas or norm-based averages of per pupil expenditures should not be applied to all or individual schools in a system, a state, or a nation. Such approaches ensure that half of the schools are below average—and half are above—for no good reasons! The staff needs to be as specific as possible in describing its objectives in performance terms and to collect data regularly and systematically so that these matters can be related to the use of money and other structural elements of education. Such responsibilities, plus opportunities for increases, provide motivation.

The Concept of Options

How students, teachers, and supervisor-managers use the elements of time, numbers, spaces, educational supplies and equipment, and money determines the excellence of a school. The emphasis has to be on how these matters affect the teaching-learning process. The data that the school collects should show specific outcomes in improved learning, teaching, and supervision-management.

Some school districts because of unusually abundant natural resources, the location of mammoth industrial or business facilities, the presence of other wealth, or the desire to build monuments may wish to spend more money on schools that this program requires. That option does exist and may be utilized so long as the other requirements of this design are provided. Certainly there are analogies in other aspects of life: for example, parks, monuments, museums, or government office buildings.

The argument in this chapter is not against luxury or beauty. However, such options must be secondary in importance to the quality of the school program. Pride of physical arrangements does not automatically improve self-concepts and learning.

The chapter that follows this one has more to say about school buildings and grounds, as well as other aspects of the environment.

Some Possible First Steps
for School Persons

1. After presentations and discussions about the use of the structural elements, the staff may select some program change that by consensus seems worth initiating. Any element in the school design would be suitable. An appropriate person(s) would then analyze what the changes would involve in the areas of time, spaces, sup-

plies and equipment, and money. Referrals would be made to the staff for discussions about what might be eliminated or changed in present practices in the areas of structural elements. The staff should also consider how to evaluate the effects of the change, using techniques described in Chapter 14.

2. The first step is a "talk and paper" operation. This second step would be to implement the change in reality and then to evaluate the results.

3. Select some area of the building, possibly the entire structure, that presently is unused or underused. Arrive at consensus for better use of the space for a specifically stated purpose. Have some competent person(s) provide cost and other factors involved in rehabilitation.

   Similar procedures could be used for reexamining use of school grounds or community areas, keeping in mind security against the risks of instrusions, vandalism, robberies, and other possible rip-offs.

For Parents and Others

1. These elements of time, numbers, spaces, supplies, equipment, and money apply to persons, families, and a variety of organizations and activities touching all aspects of life. As background for yourself and your group, select some part of your own life to analyze along the lines of this chapter and to make recommendation(s) and some positive change(s).

2. Use that background as a basis for working with school persons to analyze the school's use of the materiality of education.

12
Functional School Appearance

How can the school building and grounds relate better to homes and communities? What facilities does a school require for study, work, and conferences? How may presentations and discussions be helped by specially designed facilities? What other features help to make the building and grounds more serviceable, attractive, efficient, and economical? How is the cooperative use of facilities by schools, home, and community improved?

THE trouble with most schools is that they look like schools. Their roots are in the past when windows were the main source of light and ventilation. Other characteristics that have given the school its present-day image include:

- The central position of a teacher standing in front of acquiescent students lined up in rows of relatively uniform, often uncomfortable seats.

- The offices of the supervisory-management team are at the front entrance isolated from the rest of the building, assuming that most contacts are with the public outside.

- The teacher's "office" is in a classroom, which means it has to be empty when the teacher has a free period — or else, the teacher has no place to go except a faculty lounge.

- Most of the books are in a large library where they are guarded carefully by the person in charge.

- The largest square footage allocated to any department is for physical education because there have to be enough seats for the spectators who attend the eight or nine home basketball games held there during the year.

- If an auditorium is provided, the architectural style copies motion picture theaters or civic music halls.

- The grounds are influenced principally by the dimensions of football and other playing fields with the necessary spectator accommodations.

The whole establishment is supposed to serve neighborhood, community, or city pride, a place that illustrates outstanding interest in education. That impressive purpose gives rise to what is called the "edifice complex": if it is new and large and costs a lot of money, it has to be good.

The school building and its grounds, whether new or old, need to contrast sharply with the foregoing images. Their beauty should be in form and function. Comfort inside comes from climate control and a variety of furnishings. Utility results from numerous kinds of places for working and learning, listening and interacting, and as the building and grounds serve other needs that an urban, suburban, small town or rural area requires.

The school building reflects the concept that the home and community are complementary learning environments. The school uses them and they utilize the school. The total complex should reflect the need to provide the best possible environment for students, teachers, and the supervisory-management team to interact with each other and with persons in the area with the help of a variety of material aids.

Even if the building is new, it is never finished. It evolves continuously as a constant search is made for better ways to serve students and the area population.

The same philosophy applies equally to school supplies and equipment. The school does not, for example, replicate the up-to-date supplies and equipment of automotive and other centers in the community. Conversely, the community does not need to replicate recreational facilities that are available in the school building and on its grounds, often not used after school hours. In some settings, such use requires police protection and other security measures needed wherever people gather. However, such measures are reduced when school programs serve everyone better and more humanely.

Functions and Locations

The major portion of the building comprises study, work, and conference areas for students and teachers. The major subject fields have specialized areas. In larger schools these areas serve only one subject, while in smaller schools, with fewer students involved, two or more of the subject areas may be combined.

Each area is relatively large. Dividers, however, break up the open spaces so that students can work on learning packages or study guides, either individually or in groups of two or more. Such partial or total dividers also provide walls for students and teachers to display materials and otherwise decorate the areas. Carpeting, like the dividers, helps to keep conversational and work sounds reasonably low.

Nearby are small conference rooms where up to 20 students can gather voluntarily or are scheduled for a variety of small group activities. At central locations, in some cases serving two or more of the subject-centered areas are motivational places where audiovisual devices are used extensively. Also included in these study areas are small rooms for conferences among teachers, instruction assistants, and students on a one-to-one or at most two or three-person basis.

At various locations in the school, also convenient to the study areas, there are offices for each teacher to work, hold conferences with advisees, and perform other professional duties. Some schools put teachers of the same subject together while other schools integrate the subject areas. There is no preferred way. Since subject matter teachers also serve as teacher advisers, and thus are in touch with all of the other subject areas, the school design described here favors the subject-centered teacher offices so that it is easier for teachers to confer about their subject-centered duties. The teacher-adviser function calls less frequently for conferences with teachers in other departments.

Since the principal and assistant principals devote most of their time to working with teachers and students on the improvement of instruction, their offices should be in the same general area as the study and work centers for students and teachers. Most parent conferences about student progress are held in these areas, another reason why principals and assistant principals should be located there.

Other supervisor-manager team members, except for department chairpersons, have their offices located near the main entrance of the school for the convenience of visitors. Those persons who actually need to see the principal, an assistant principal, or department head are directed to them by the receptionist who helps each visitor to determine who can provide the assistance needed. The other S-M team members, near the main entrance on the first floor are readily accessible to most of the persons who need to see them. The process and the office locations thus help public relations and save time for all S-M team members.

Where Students Learn

The work and activity centers for the various subjects are located around the periphery of the building, close to the outdoors. Students engaged in study activities may walk to a window for a brief change of scenery when the need arises. Science needs special places for animals and plants to grow and for the conduct of experiments where safety and protection are significant elements. The noise factors that occur in the subject areas of health-fitness-recreation, practical arts, and fine arts make it advisable to locate these activities near to each other and away from areas that need more quiet.

Meetings of small groups after large-group presentations are held in conference rooms adjacent to the study and work centers. Interior rooms are preferred for these meetings because exterior rooms often present distractions.

The building also provides teaching auditoriums for motivational presentations. The principal difference between a teaching auditorium and conventional ones used for concerts, dramatic presentations, and speakers is the general shape of the facility. Some conventional school auditoriums are relatively level and have seats uniformly facing the front instead of focusing on the center stage. The audience space is unnecessarily large. Such auditoriums are not ideal.

The maximum desirable seating capacity of school auditoriums should be about 500 to 600. Programs should be repeated if more than that number need accommodations. The slope of the floor from front to back is equivalent to that from a first floor to a third floor level. Such a slope, with all seats focusing on the stage, helps the audience to see and understand the presentation. In larger schools where more motivational presentations occur each week, movable presentations in the auditorium permit three groups to meet simultaneously.

These presentation areas need the best possible equipment to enable everyone to see and hear well, not only for the motivational presentations but also for fine and speech arts programs. The teaching auditorium described here is especially suited for these school programs because everyone in the audience has a good seat. It is better to repeat performances if more people want to see them, an experience that the participants enjoy. If there is a special occasion for gathering a large audience, it is more economical for the school to rent a public place. School auditoriums must be teaching facilities.

General Considerations

Improving a school's cafeteria can be done in many ways. Certainly the food service facility should be open for longer periods of time to avoid the great onrush of students during the middle of the day. Already one large city school cafeteria serves breakfast with many lunch periods and afternoon snacks, a good practice. Also, the cavernous cafeteria should be replaced by a number of smaller rooms, each with a particular type of setting and supervision. Some areas are relatively small and quiet while others are somewhat larger. Art and home economic classes plan and execute the decor.

The cafeteria in this *school for everyone* is not a place where students of necessity eat what the home economics department and others have been unable to interest students in doing, namely, to eat a balanced lunch. Students have a wide variety of choices in what they eat in the cafeteria. Some areas even specialize in gourmet cooking, the work being done partly by students who are interested in the art as a hobby and by others who wish to pursue it vocationally. As is the case with other facilities, the cafeteria serves community needs, e.g. lunches for senior citizens.

A number of other general features in the building need attention. Year-round programs require year-round air conditioning. The use of glass in schools needs to be compromised—not so much of it as in the "greenhouse-effect" that was popular for many decades in the mid-twentieth century and not so little as in the "windowless" schools built by some architects in the 1960s. Small windows should be placed in strategic positions so that the people inside the building may readily determine the condition of the weather outside and to rest their eyes by occasionally looking at more distant vistas and attractive plantings that specially interested students develop.

Careful planning of access routes within the school largely eliminates conventional unproductive and costly institutional-type corridor spaces. Study and work areas also economize on space as compared with traditional classrooms that have aisles, teacher areas in front, and other relatively unused spaces. Of course, all these improvements and other changes must be in accord with fire and building codes or other legal constraints. Sometimes outmoded regulations need updating.

Transferring appropriate study and work activities from the school building to homes and the community reduces the size of buildings in relation to pupil enrollment, thus also providing savings.

The general atmosphere of the school is improved with its carpeted floors and its student and faculty involvement in decorating their spaces. Plants and flowers should be around not only as a part of the horticultural work of the school but also for the general interest that young people, teachers, and community adults have in living things. Students enjoy plants and react positively to them as do adults. Creative arrangements thus produce a pleasant place where people can enjoy studying, working, and learning together not only in comfort but with obvious pleasure in doing so.

This kind of atmosphere generates a camaraderie that is inspirational. The school is a place where people of all ages are welcome. Thus it truly becomes a public service institution that enhances community interest and support. This school environment actually produces better attendance, fewer discipline problems, and higher levels of scholarship and achievement than the conventional institutionalized approach where some teachers and students seem to be involved in a continual, competitive game. The few students who cannot (or at the time will not) function properly in such an environment, are changed to a different place: the school's close supervision area or to the community, as determined by each one's teacher adviser.

Outside the School Building

The school grounds should resemble a park, with a variety of playing areas and outdoor facilities. One school known to this writer had a shallow pond with plants, fish, and water fowl. Students and staff alike enjoyed it as well as an adjacent park that combined the natural environment of the area in which the school was located. The facility was used by school departments and also by adults.

The school grounds need to be a living laboratory for many of the school subject fields. The obvious example is for the physical and biological sciences; but this design also extends to the fine arts, the practical arts, English, social studies, and in fact, all subject fields. The grounds can become an exciting place for everyone, used both by students and adults.

The separation of park boards and school boards and similar groups is an unfortunate development. We can hope, however, that they will schedule many cooperative activities.

Supplies and Equipment

Furnishing the school with the tools of teaching and learning should be a gradual and never-ending process. Present budgetary procedures operational in many school districts need to be changed in order to make funds available continuously for the purchase of supplies and equipment as the program develops rather than requiring massive expenditures as a part of construction costs. Spreading expenditures over longer periods of time helps to create the image of an evolving school that is never completely finished.

Another important process with respect to educational materials is to involve the community in planning and conducting the educational program. The school design emphasizes an enlightened and cooperative relationship with the community. Included is having students use supplies and equipment located in the community as well as in the school.

The conventional approach has been simply to ask everyone in the community to pay taxes which the school then spent to meet its own purposes. An on-going, continued relationship in which communities and schools share appropriately produces better utilization of supplies and equipment. For example, offices, garages, stores, and the like have profit motives to keep modernizing. Students whose advisers arrange for them to study and work there benefit from those experiences. If the school purchases some new equipment that the others do not have, cooperative programs make it available to them. There are realistic values in the closer relationships among home, school, and community.

The Evolving School

Teachers, administrators, and influential community members change their ideas about education from time to time. Students differ about what they want to learn and how they should learn it. Educational research and development authorities recommend novel approaches to schooling. Shortages in supplies over which the school system has no control or the discovery of new methods of heating, lighting, ventilation, and the like may make alterations in existing buildings desirable. Since a school is never finished, future needs for change must be anticipated by ease of remodeling.

How to provide for flexibility brought some problems in the past; for example, a decade or more ago the reaction that some architects had to the concept of flexibility was to provide movable walls. Unfortunately, these walls were not always satisfactory from the standpoint of sound control, and they sometimes interfered with proper ventilation and lighting. What was really needed were walls that could be changed from time to time with relatively little costs as the needs of a program changed. Seldom does a wall need to be moved immediately. In most instances, a few days' or a weekend's notice could be given.

Multi-purpose spaces in a school also represent a poor solution to the need for flexibility. This concept has made audiovisual presentations in conventional classrooms unsatisfactory. Carpeting all rooms is also unsatisfactory; some should have hard surface floors. Conversely, hard surface flooring in all rooms interferes with audio presentations. Also, such rooms are noisier than they need to be since students and teachers converse frequently.

Those persons who plan buildings and grounds, including architects, need to keep in mind how these facilities will be changed as educational needs evolve over the years. We restate an important design concept made earlier in this chapter. School buildings and the grounds are never completed. They must evolve with the changing times so that the ideas that students, teachers, supervisor-managers, and

159

community persons develop may be incorporated with reasonable costs and efforts.

How does this *school for everyone* determine when changes in educational facilities—or any other aspect of a school—are needed? What kinds of data are needed, and what methods are used? Such needs call for different approaches to evaluating present programs, the subject of Chapter 14. Closely related, however, are the techniques that schools use to evaluate pupil progress—the subject of the chapter that follows this one.

Some Possible First Steps for School Persons

1. Survey students, teachers, and supervisor-managers to solicit inadequacies or other problems with the existing school and grounds. At the same time ask for suggestions on ways to improve the situation.

2. Select some part of the design for school improvement from other chapters in order to relate the needs for that change to the data collected under the foregoing survey.

3. Analyze how the proposals for increased use of homes and the community as study and work centers, plus changes in utilization of space in the present building, could provide savings to be used for better school facilities.

4. If parts of the present building—or even a total building—are now unused because of declining school enrollments, investigate how community groups or private enterprises might use these facilities in return for which they could contribute funds or services that would help the school.

For Parents and Others

1. Analyze how the existing facilities for teaching and learning in homes and the community duplicate unnecessarily the school facilities—or are unused to some extent because of existing school or community policies.

2. Conduct a survey among persons in homes and community establishments to discover possible interests in and ideas about how they might better utilize school facilities.

3. Use the data from these studies in meetings with school officials to explore the possibilities of joint efforts to improve educational facilities for everyone.

13
Evaluating
Pupil Progress

What are the limitations of single letter grades—even with pluses and minuses? How does a school indicate how far a student has progressed in all subjects? How does the school show how a student compares with others? How does the school describe the unique things that each student has accomplished? What options are available to the students?

PRESENT systems of appraising and reporting pupil progress are at best inadequate and at times represent a comedy of errors with tragic consequences. Schools maintain these methods largely because colleges use them. Despite low levels of reliability and validity, the system persists.

Prospective employers consider carefully the letter grades that high school students receive because that is all the schools provide in any systematic way. Parents, products of the system and unaware of options, support the program and in fact resist changes in it. They fear they will not understand a new system.

Teachers and school administrators, also products of the letter-grade system, are comfortable with it and hesitate to change; moreover, they have had personally rewarding experiences with it by successfully completing their own school and university programs.

Students themselves have personal biases. Many of them, especially those who receive good marks, defend the system for many of the same reasons.

Present Grading Systems

Criticisms of the A B C D F or other similar marking systems are frequent, however. Instead of summarizing and repeating all the faults that generations of writers have pointed out, let's look at six shortcomings of grading and reporting practices. They provide background for the appraisal system described in this book.

First, the present system is based mainly upon competition among students rather than on measuring progress of individual students. Although there is nothing wrong with competition, emphasizing a competitive marking system ignores the basic needs for individual appraisal as described later. The argument that "life is that way" scarcely applies here.

The real world sorts human beings into a variety of social, economic, and occupational groups whereas the school puts all of them together into one competitive system. Competition is a reasonable motivational device only when the participants have a chance to win; for many students that chance is minimal with resultant frustration.

A second fault arises from the reason for continuing the letter grade system. School officials like the system because it facilitates the calculation of rank-in-class, information that university admission officers often request, employers seek, and schools themselves use to select winners of scholarships and to determine eligibility of students participating in interscholastic competitions. The practice springs from ease of calculation rather than educationally sound purposes. The reason actually is spurious because it is possible with other procedures to appraise pupil progress for ranking purposes, based on how each student grows and develops.

A third deficiency of the ABCDF system is that letter grades are based almost completely on learning prescribed knowledge and skills. Such goals as creativity, desirable attitudes, application of knowledge to new situations, and other so-called affective goals are not reported. When accomplishments in the affective domains are included, it is often an afterthought used to shade a grade one step higher or lower on the basis of some attitude or effort that the student demonstrates.

Schools thus rate outcomes in the affective area as unimportant, when realistically, success in employment or in living styles is greatly influenced by superiority in these areas. The successful person does not represent a dichotomy between thinking and feeling on the one hand and memorizing and doing on the other. Rather, everyone is a synthesis of values and achievements.

A fourth limitation of conventional marking systems is that they ignore unique student achievements—outcomes that usually tell more about total personality than does attaining the common knowledge, understandings, and skills expected of all students. The special projects or studies not required of everyone may lead to careers or hobbies that enrich the individual's life. To ignore such accomplishments, as the conventional letter grade system typically does—or at least pays relatively little attention to—again violates the principle of individuality and rewards conformity to general goals.

A fifth shortcoming of the ABCDF system is that it is the simpliest and least time-consuming method for computing grades. Since schools do not provide teachers with enough time to develop comprehensive systems of appraising and recording pupil progress, they take the easiest method. As a result, teachers are not stimulated to think more deeply about the relationships between the appraisal system and what will be most beneficial to each student in terms of future studies, work, and hobbies.

The sixth fault is that single letter grades serve too well the simplistic demands of colleges, employers, and parents. They understand it, they are accustomed to it, and they like it. Are these reasons sufficiently sound for using a system that is less productive of continued learnings than it might be?

The background of what is wrong with current evaluating and reporting practices provides clues to what schools need to do to improve the system. The design for the school recommended here accepts some aspects of the old system, but puts them into proper relationship to other procedures that tell people more of what they need to know and how to use the data.

The Proposed System

The aim in evaluating and reporting progress in the *school for everyone* is to help each student improve, regardless of potential and aptitudes. The method is a continuing, evolving one that goes beyond merely reporting achievement at a given time.

The goals of the evaluation process are to produce data that will help the student, teacher, or the parent, to diagnose the present situation accurately, to examine possible ways to improve, to assist in selecting the specific steps to implement, and then to evaluate further. Also, to be revealed are possible career and enriching interests or hobbies. The student is not a mere observer in the procedure but an active participant.

To achieve these goals, the system needs to tell:

1) where the student is at a given time in the continuum of learning;

2) how the individual compares with other students; and

3) what the student has done that was *not* required.

Although these three elements are interrelated, they have to be considered as discrete parts. The person who reads the report, including the student, will make the obvious interrelationships.

The *first* includes an appraisal and report of what the student has completed in all of the areas of the curriculum as described in Chapter 6. When the student completes required items in a curriculum sequence, that fact is recorded. A document accompanying the report indicates the nature of these items and the criteria for measuring achievement. Therefore, what is reported is the quantity of work completed at the specified quality level that the school requires. Thus, the person reading the report knows how far the student has gone in mathematics, social studies, fine arts, and all of the other areas of study.

The *second* part of the reporting system shows the student's performance on norm-based instruments. For example, the report shows such information as the following: scores on standardized reading examinations; number of error-free words per minute that the student is able to type with standards provided for comparisons; performance by standardized measures in running or other aspects of health, fitness, and recreation; and many others in all subject fields.

Again, an accompanying document indicates the nature of the instruments that the school has administered along with the norms for the local school and the city, state, or nation, as available. These data provide the student and

Where Am I?

PROGRESS IN
LEARNING
SEQUENCE

Number recognition | Multiplication | Algebraic equations | Calculus

How Do I Compare?

NORM-BASED
ACHIEVEMENT
[DATE AND
MEASURE GIVEN]

0   50   100

PERCENTILE

What Have I Done?

SPECIAL
ACHIEVEMENT
NOT REQUIRED
OF EVERYONE

SUBJECT:	Activity:_____
	_____
	Performance:_____
	_____
DATE:	Product:_____

167

other interested persons with a basis of comparison. Carefully written statements indicate how to interpret these data, their limitations, and values. For example, there could be an indication that these tests typically reflect the socio-economic status of the locale—and often the individual.

Keeping these data from students, their parents, and other persons who need them is indefensible. If a school system is unwilling to release these data, the school should not administer the tests. Of course, specialized instruments given only to selected students for specific purposes should not be included in reports that go to everyone.

The *third* part of the reporting system shows what the student has accomplished that was *not* required. Examples include completing advanced reading in English, doing special projects in science, participating in interscholastic or intramural football activities, completing a specified project in the community, work experience, and the like.

This information, in reality, is the most significant aspect of the appraisal and reporting system because it describes the student as a unique person, showing both special interests and talents. The descriptive statement for each activity is brief, indicating what was done, where, and how much time was spent. Most schools probably would add some qualitative evaluation but it is not necessary to do so. An interested person could ascertain further details either by talking or writing directly to the student or by contacting his or her teacher, employer, or supervisor.

Reasons for Change

Combined, the foregoing three elements provide a complete description of a student so far as the school is able to assemble. The emphasis is on individual accomplishments although the second part of the report provides comparative data.

Failures are not reported in this program. The purpose of the school is not to produce failures but to develop each individual student to the maximum degree possible in terms of interest and competencies. Most of all, this report describes positively the individual accomplishments, emphasizes special things done, and defines more accurately the unique personality of the student.

Such a reporting system provides universities, or any other schools to which the student might transfer, much more information than does the conventional transfer of credits. Selection of students for whatever purpose is more meaningful under this process than through the conventional rank-in-class. Personnel officers can relate students better to specific jobs than by merely using criteria like high school graduation, rank-in-class, and grades earned in a typing course.

The report specified in this design for a school provides students with better information to use in conferences with parents, school and college officials, and prospective employers. The conventional reporting system leaves so much unsaid that the student often is at a loss to explain the meaning of some grades. No wonder that students facing potential employers or admissions officers can often only vaguely answer or rationalize explanations.

This appraisal and reporting system places more responsibilities and opportunities on the school than do conventional grading and reporting systems. Obviously, such a program requires more time, increased care in appraisal and record-keeping, and the necessity of more options to students so that they have opportunities to develop reports that are as complimentary as possible.

The preparation of these reports constitutes a high level of professional action for teachers. The differentiated staff provides time and assistance. Each teacher adviser assembles the reports for his or her advisees.

Another essential of the design calls for proper uses of data processing. Subject teachers report students' completion of curriculum segments to the teacher adviser via computer printouts. Other reports show completion and resultant data from standardized or other norm-based and criterion-referenced evaluations. Computer printouts also describe the special or unusual things that each student completes in a school or in the community.

The final report does not look like the report cards and cummulative records that schools use today. *Dossier* is a better word to describe it. Students then could add their own appraisals and rationalizations of why the reports are as they are—properly identified and signed by them.

The design calls for a high level of professional activity on the part of both school personnel and persons outside the school who have need to know about students. But it is relatively fruitless to improve other aspects of education without also changing the kind and amount of data for appraising and reporting student progress. Moreover, these data are essential to provide better diagnoses of pupil needs.

Options in the System

In harmony with what has been said elsewhere in this book, the school also needs to provide options in the appraisal and reporting system. A student has a right to ask what grade would have been given on a traditional report card. Parents or others might ask the same question. The school has little difficulty in simply answering a C, or whatever the case might be.

School personnel should also be prepared to provide comparative data when required to do so by students, parents, or prospective employers or colleges, being sure to indicate the limitations of such data in terms of reliability and validity. For example, the completion of a given number of segments in a course could be expressed as tenths of a conventional unit of credit—instead of giving a failing grade for an entire course.

Similarly, the school provides conventional rank-in-class and/or a diploma for a student—not automatically but on the request of a bonafide person or institutional representative. The school official responsible for those activities considers all the data for all students and produces diplomas and comparative rank-in-class that are in fact just as valid and reliable—probably more so—as the usual procedures of adding up grade points. The method simply involves using the available data that the school has for all the graduates or students at a given year in school, separating the students into decile groups, and assigning the ranks.

A careful statement of the reasons for not following conventional schemes all the time for all the students should be made. Insisting on the same program, forced arbitrarily upon everyone, is not the benchmark of an enlightened institution. Carefully developed explanations of the reasons for change are essential. The need also exists, especially in periods of transition, to permit options. Most persons are reasonable and will recognize the superiority of individualized appraisal when they understand its advantages and works. However, the options are present.

The Emphasis Here Is Deliberate

The image of the school is created in many ways. An appraisal and reporting system with a positive approach to help each person constitutes one of the most important aspects of the program. Building confident and yet realistic self-images of students results from a more humane environment. That approach rather than "putting them down" is the goal for all students.

A *school for everyone* differs in many ways from schools that cater to highly motivated and able students on the one hand and to deprived, underachievers on the other. The great majority of students in most schools fall into neither category.

What do schools do for them? What is the excitement in a grade of C—or a rank of 191 in a class of 326 members? What truly creative activities that a student achieves are buried in that grade of C?

Isn't it time that schools do something constructive about unjust practices that fail to motivate, in fact, turn-off young people? The grading system is high on the list of offenders in most schools. The design proposed here can attack these problems constructively.

Next in this book are some other ideas about evaluation. In this case the reference is to the total program of the school. How good is it? How may it be improved?

Some Possible First Steps for School Persons

1. Supplement the present marking system by providing students and their parents with a brief statement, for example, on a 3" × 5" form, evaluating a special project or activity that a student has completed. Maintain a carbon copy that can be used in a summary report at the end of a course or year.

2. As a first step in acquainting students and parents with a more descriptive report card, supplement the letter grade (or whatever you are using) with two or more statements and a check mark as illustrated in this example:

Activity	Frequency		
	Almost always	Some of the time	Almost never
Does more work than the minimum required			
Makes positive suggestions to others in the class for improving their work			
Add others:			

3. Release to each student and the parents the data from some standardized test that the school had administered to all or most students with an explanation of what the instrument aims to show, the individual's score, and an indication on a check list of what that score might mean for the student.

For Parents and Others

1. Develop personally, or with others, a statement about the kind of information and data that you would like to receive from the school.

2. How would you like to have the data reported?

3. What data, if any, should be confidential?

14

Determining Program Values

Why do schools need different and more comprehensive methods for judging the quality of their programs? How well do the persons involved understand what they are attempting to accomplish and how committed are they? How may school persons judge degrees of progress in reaching the objectives? What consequences does the program produce for students, teachers, and supervisor-managers? How does a school make the best use of program evaluation?

THE methods generally used in judging schools are not adequate—neither for conventional schools, nor for schools that offer more individualized programs. Criteria now used by many state departments of education, regional accrediting agencies, and university admissions officers have little or no basis in research. The public needs help in evaluating school excellence.

The standard criteria used for rating the quality of schools include measures such as teacher-pupil ratios, expenditures per pupil, average years of preparation of teachers, number of minutes per week that classes meet, expenditures for

174

school supplies and equipment, newness of buildings, the presence of certain course requirements for graduation, the number of years that students spend in school, success of students in interscholastic competitions, how well students score on reading and other norm-based tests, the number of publications by faculty members, and degrees of satisfaction with existing programs.

Many of these items are influenced positively by the financial affluence of the community and the socioeconomic and cultural status and mores of the people who live there. These criteria almost automatically help some schools to present an image of success. So, why change?

Metropolitan schools are frequently judged by the number of robberies, extortions, and the degrees of danger in coming to and leaving the building, and while in it, the extent of drug sales on campus and similar concerns. Those problems also occur to some degree in other schools. Parents, teachers, students, as well as other community persons give the administration and the program bad marks when such conditions are allowed to persist.

Should school authorities be blamed for external, societal conditions, many of which are beyond their control? What else makes program evaluation difficult?

Emphasizing comparisons among schools on regional or national bases is unwise for a number of reasons. Schools in this country legally are creatures of the state. State legislatures pass laws which state departments of education interpret and enforce. Prescriptions include curriculum subject and topic requirements, textbook selection, amount of state financial aid, requirements for teacher certification, and a host of other matters. There could be 50 different ideas about the functions of schools which, therefore, influence programs and their evaluations.

Even comparing schools within a state is difficult. In reality, much control over schools is vested in local school districts. The local schools are subject to a variety of pressures which members of local governing boards exert and have the legal right to enforce. Board members may represent pressure groups with selfish interests. They may also sometimes push programs that are personal hobbies.

Employees of school systems and other influential groups also have special goals that affect evaluation. Teacher organizations want higher pay, shorter hours, and smaller classes. School administrators want more security and influence, and fewer problems. Some students want more freedom; others want less.

In addition, taxpayers who have little or no control over other government expenditures express themselves vigorously when the annual school budget is presented for review. University professors sometimes look upon the schools as a source of their own survival by insisting that their subject is more important than others; therefore, they rate schools on that basis. Suppliers of school equipment and materials may exert all sorts of pressures to obtain more sales and profits.

Unfortunately, no specific rules exist at state or national levels to assist school administrators in coping with the foregoing demands sometimes made by special interest groups and individuals—and which affect the quality of the program one way or another. Although it is difficult to develop a simple method for evaluation of educational programs, something has to be done. Conventional methods do not assure basic improvements in schools; sometimes they interfere.

How Good Is a School?

Students, parents, and taxpayers all ask about educational quality. Even those with little interest in education want to know if their school enhances the community's image. University admissions officers and employers, too, need to determine how well a student is prepared to achieve in their institutions.

The question has two dimensions: how good is the school today compared to yesterday and how does it compare with other schools? Both are reasonable, but in most cases the questions have not received reliable and valid answers.

One other dimension is essential. What data are needed to diagnose what needs to be done to improve the program, to help decide what prescriptive actions should be implemented in anticipation of further evaluations? The goal, of course, is a better basis than schools now have for making program changes.

The design for evaluation in this *school for everyone* also applies to all kinds of schools in various environments that serve all ages and types of students. All schools need the following data:

- degrees of *understanding* and *commitment* to the stated purposes of the school's program;
- analyses of *criterion-referenced data* in relation to the stated program objectives;
- degrees of *progress toward the stated purposes* of the school;
- *program consequences* for students, teachers, and the supervisory-management team;
- performance on *norm-based instruments;* and
- *opinions* of visiting experts and program participants.

1. Understanding and Commitment

Every school has some kind of program design. For evaluation purposes, it matters not whether the program is viewed as *conventional* or *innovative* in total concept or in specified parts. How well students, teachers, members of the supervisory-management team in the school, central office personnel, and other members of the community *understand* the program is important in the evaluation technique recommended here. Related is how much *commitment* they have to the basic concepts that the school has developed for its program.

Although it is possible to develop instruments for statewide or national use, it is better for local school improvement to use ones with a vocabulary that may be more clearly understood in the vicinity.

One kind of data reflects the perceptions of members of the school community regarding the changes in teacher and student roles as specified by the program, in this case, of the *school for everyone*. On a continuum from zero to nine inclusive, each group indicates, for example, whether a teacher or student: *never* performs in a manner as described (0), *always performs* (9), or *about half the time* (4) or (5). Here are three sample items:

Teacher questions call for responses by students that involve higher levels of thinking than merely memorizing information.	0 1 2 3 4 5 6 7 8 9
Teacher advisers help students to prepare their schedules.	0 1 2 3 4 5 6 7 8 9
Teacher efforts result in every student making progress in achieving desirable learning outcomes.	0 1 2 3 4 5 6 7 8 9

Another part of this evaluation asks for a direct *yes, no,* or *don't know* response to such statements as the following:

In this school teachers have paid clerical assistants.	Yes	No	Don't Know
Learning prescriptions for students include listening to tape recordings.	Yes	No	Don't Know
Professional counselors make up student programs.	Yes	No	Don't Know

A third section calls for *agree, disagree,* or *uncertain* responses to these illustrative statements:

178

Students are too much on their own with too little help from teachers.	Agree	Disagree	Uncertain
Learning improves more as students are told specifically about their mistakes rather than giving them failing grades.	Agree	Disagree	Uncertain
Teachers spend too much time in their offices, away from students.	Agree	Disagree	Uncertain

Such statements illustrate three lists that teachers and the supervisory-management team need to develop. The data produced by the responses of the different groups: (1) show their understanding of and commitment to what is going on in the school and (2) provide a basis for diagnosing what needs to be done next so that prescriptive actions may be implemented. Repetition of the study a semester or year later, or at whatever interval of time is selected, provides both present program evaluation and suggestions for continued efforts to improve.

2. Criterion-Referenced Data

The school has established what it expects to accomplish by a specified time and the means to do so. Such criteria represent local definitions that students, teachers, parents and others understand and accept. Program objectives defined in specific, performance terms provide a basis for the school to measure how well the program achieves the purposes at the time the evaluation is made. The aim then is either to change the objectives or to plan how to achieve the goals.

The following sample statements illustrate purposes and measures to use in this part of the evaluation:

Program Objective	*Illustrative Measures*
Independent learning activities outside of the school are being used by students.	Records of outside student learning activities (e.g., work experience, studies in libraries and/or museums, advanced placement, work as teacher assistants, community service, etc.) show where, when, and accomplishments.

179

Teachers are released from specified clerical duties and routine supervision of pupils to provide time, energy, and facilities so they may prepare, perform and evaluate better; advise students; develop curriculum materials; analyze needs and develop professional solutions.

Students move through the school's required learnings at rates optimal for each individual.

Surveys indicate that teachers spend _____% of their time developing curriculum materials; _____% of time advising and directing students; _____% of time analyzing needs and developing professional solutions; and _____% of time on clerical duties and routine supervision of pupils.

A random sample of 50 students, more or less, in a given subject or area of learning, shows the amount of differentiation of progress in learning rates among them.

3. Degrees of Progress Toward the Total Design

This form of program evaluation is similar to the methods traditionally used by state departments of education and regional accrediting associations; only the stated goals and measures are different. The basic aim, however, is not to compare one school with another, but rather for one school to plot its progress toward the goals which the staff has established and local governing bodies have accepted.

Traditionally, such evaluation would concern matters like the percent of teachers having master's degrees, the number of minutes classes meet each week, or the number of books in the library. Now the aim is different. How well has the school reached its prescribed goals of services through instructional assistants, clerical assistants, and general aides, changes in how students spend time in school, and other matters that this design prescribes?

The following samples illustrate some kinds of data the *school for everyone* uses to measure progress:

Indicate from 0% to 100% in This School the Progress in Reaching Goals: (the goal described in this book is 100% under items 1 and 2, 0% under No.3):

1. Degree to which all pupils have systematic, continual contact *weekly* with curriculum areas:

Subject Area	Percent
1. English	_____
2. Fine Arts	_____
3. Health, Fitness, Recreation (PE)	_____
4. Mathematics	_____

180

5. Other Cultures (For. Lang.)   ——————
6. Practical Arts   ——————
7. Religion (Parochial)   ——————
8. Science   ——————
9. Social Studies   ——————

2. Each teacher has a private or semi-private office   ——————

3. Percent of students that received one or more F (failure) grades for the semester or most recent reports   ——————

4. *Program Consequences for Students, Teachers, and Supervisor-Managers*

The data described under the three previous categories indicate how well the program is understood and how committed the participants are to it, the extent to which specified criteria or program aspects are being achieved, and a definite indication of what is currently happening in relation to *all* of the specified goals. The fourth type of data show how the program affects the behavior of students, teachers, and supervisor-managers. These data serve as a further check on the other findings as well as indications for further procedures.

All school persons stop at randomly selected signals to record: what each one of them is doing; where, why, and with whom; values and outcomes; and personal feelings. Separate but quite similar forms are checked four or more times a day for a week by students, teachers, and supervisor-managers. Provisions are made for one or more activities that occur outside the regular hours of the school day. The whole process should be repeated at least two times during each year.

The school may use a sample of students for the analyses but all staff members are included in the tabulations. The data for teachers are combined for tabulation on a departmental basis. Data for students are combined in terms of years in school. The supervisory-management team is considered as a unit. The purpose obviously is not to analyze individual performance but rather the departmental group, various categories of students, and the total program of supervision.

The emphasis, constantly repeated, is that the data are *not* used to compare individuals with other persons, or one school with another school, but rather to assure the continuous process of program improvement. Further diagnoses, selection of prescriptive actions that are then implemented and further appraised in the same way constitute the purposes and the process.

The charts that follow indicate *only* partial lists of representative items to illustrate what has been used successfully in a variety of types of schools and locations:

REPRESENTATIVE ITEMS

Student Log Form	*Teacher Log Form*
What	**Activity**
Work/Community experience	Advising/Counseling
Science	Presenting (motivation)
Discipline/Detention	Supervising (overseeing)
etc. as listed	Evaluating program
	Conversing informally
Where	Doing clerical work
Home	etc. as listed
School	
Community	**With Whom**
	Self
Activity	Students
Listening to teacher	Teachers
Reading	School administrators/supervisors
Memorizing	Parents
Waiting	Community resource people
Making something	etc. as listed
etc. as listed	
	How Many With You
Why	Alone
Assigned by teacher	1
My own choice	2-4
	5-15
Type	etc. as listed
Subject related	
Not subject related	**Where**
	School
How Many	Home
1 (just myself)	Community
2-6	etc. as listed
7-15	
etc. as listed	

Help
  Teacher
  Other student

Value To Me
  High
  Medium
  Low

What Happened
  Put to use something I learned
  Made me think differently
  Helped someone or the school
  Nothing
  etc. as listed

Feeling
  Enjoyed doing something
  Did not enjoy it
  I don't know

Value To Me
  High
  Low
  None

Product
  Learning materials
  Solution to problem
  Anxiety reduction/catharsis
  Budget, policy, document
    (letter, bulletin)
  None
  etc. as listed

Perception of Effect On Others
  Stimulating
  Little or no effect
  Neither

REPRESENTATIVE ITEMS

| | | ALL GROUPS | |
		During School Day	Before or After School
	Supervisory-Management Team Form		
ACTIVITY	Developing professionally		
	Evaluating program		
	Evaluating staff		
	Negotiating		
	Doing clerical work		
	Checking on building & materials		
	Relaxing/Eating		
	Traveling from place to place		
	etc. as listed		
AREA OF CONCERN	School/Plant Management		
	Instructional Personnel		
	Community Relations		
	Curriculum and Instruction		
	Personal		
	etc. as listed		
WITH WHOM	Self		
	Students		
	Teachers		
	Other supervisory-management team		
	Salespersons		
	etc. as listed		

		During School Day	Before or After School
HOW MANY WITH YOU	Alone 1 2-4 16 or more		
WHERE	School Community Central office Other schools etc. as listed		
VALUE TO ME	High Moderate Low		
PRODUCT	Plan design Solution to problem Evaluation Input/Feedback etc. as listed		

The foregoing items represent only part of the information actually provided on the forms. Each school needs to decide what data are important for program evaluation as well as for diagnostic and prescriptive purposes.

School officials for similar reasons also need to collect, record, and analyze data like the following which relate to students, professional staff, and the community. The instructions are to circle one response that indicates the situation *now* as compared with a specified time in the past, for example, one year ago, or an average of several years.

I.   Community
1.0 P.T.A. meetings
    1.1 Attendance as compared to an average year: less   about the same   more

    1.2 Nature of meetings: e.g., interpreting the school's program: (each listed separately)   less   about the same   more

2.0 Attendance at special school events compared with an average year: less   about the same   more

2.1 Athletic contest attendance:	less	about the same	more
2.2 Music concerts attendance:	less	about the same	more

3.0 Parental concerns:

3.1 Number of phone calls or letters from parents adversely critical of the educational program: (classified by nature)	less	about the same	more
3.2 Number of phone calls or letters from parents in favor of the program: (ditto)	less	about the same	more

4.0 News media:

4.1 Number and nature of newspaper stories of the school program: _____	less	about the same	more
4.2 Number and requests to appear on radio or TV programs: _____	less	about the same	more

Etc. as listed

II. Students

10.0 Absences (various reasons)	less	about the same	more
11.0 Discipline, e.g. number of referrals as compared to normal year:	less	about the same	more

11.1 Number of suspensions, etc.: _____

12.0 Number of students with reasons for requesting a transfer to another school: _____

13.0 Number of students and reasons for dropping out of school:_____

14.0 Use of the library areas as compared to normal year:	less	about the same	more
15.0 Use of the community as a classroom as compared to a normal year:	less	about the same	more
15.1 Number of individuals (students) assigned work or study with specified outside agencies:_____	less	about the same	more

16.0 Student population changes shown by ability scores: (as listed)

17.0 Results of other standardized tests:	lower	about the same	higher

18.0 Student responsibility for learning based on   lower   about the   higher
      teacher observation: (as listed)   same

19.0 Number of seniors graduating earlier or
      later than normal (by number of semesters
        + or -)_____.

Etc. as listed

5. Use of Norm-Based Data

Evaluation also needs norm-based data that show comparisons of the school with others not necessarily committed to the same educational philosophy. However, there are important limitations in using comparative data based on city, county, state or national standards. These data tend to reflect the socioeconomic bases of communities, parental aspirations, and other mores, rather than the quality of educational programs. For example, when the nature of a school's population changes, scores on such instruments also change even though other factors remain constant.

Nevertheless, comparisons *of one point in time to another* provide leads for casual analyses. One must keep in mind, too, that these data have public relations implications. Answers to the following questions are useful: Do students read better, at the same level, or worse as measured by a standardized reading test from one time to another? What changes have occurred in pupil scores on tests in other fields such as spelling, typing speed, biology, or United States history? What factors have caused the changes?

Some schools have found interesting results after administering standardized tests in the affective areas. For example, a test of creativity administered to students whose school emphasized creative efforts revealed significantly higher scores on a norm-based test of creativity. More measurements of affective behavior are needed.

6. Evaluations by Visiting Experts and Program Participants

Visits by persons having special preparation and techniques still have a place in school evaluation. The problem with these procedures, of course, is that visitors tend to view, hear, and read according to their own backgrounds of experience. Prior to the visits, the group of observers needs common preparation, interactions to clarify procedures, and guides to add reliability to their observations.

When these visitors are prepared adequately, visit the same kinds of persons, ask comparable questions, keep the same kinds of notes, and prepare similar reports, their observations can produce comparative data to help both the school and also those persons interested in looking at several schools as guides for further improvements.

The following inquiries illustrate the kind of data gathering that should be developed cooperatively by the schools and the visiting experts:

- Is the work of teachers analyzed in order to discover what teachers *must* do and what may be done more economically yet productively by other persons and/or machines? If so, what changes resulted?

- Do teachers have time during the school day to prepare, to keep up-to-date, to develop materials for pupils in their independent study, to confer with colleagues, to work as needed with individual students, and to develop pupil evaluation techniques and reporting? Again, with what results?

- Do elementary children and secondary students have access to teachers who are knowledgeable and talented in science, music, art, foreign language, and other specialized areas so that the important concepts in these fields are learned accurately?

- Does school policy permit each pupil to proceed at his or her own pace through the learning sequences with specially prepared materials that minimize frustration or boredom? What evidence is available to show implementation?

- Does the school provide individualized instruction, i.e., continuous progress, special projects, personal scheduling, individualized evaluation? Does a staff member monitor the progress of each pupil?

- Does the school measure educational output (pupil gains) in relation to financial input (school expenditures)? How?

- What portion of the school budget is spent on research? How much on the development of new teaching methods, organization of instruction, new content, evaluation techniques, and the like? How do these data compare to previous ones in this school?

Another type of subjective evaluation of programs results from the use of opinion surveys of *present* and *former* students, teachers, members of the supervisory-management team, parents, and other community members. The staff determines what questions are asked and then provides the respondents with opportunities for free responses. The reliability and validity of these instruments is enhanced when the responses to the questions are requested in behavioral or performance terms.

Reports and Actions

Are school programs today better than a year ago? Are the programs better than what occurs in other schools?

Typically these questions have been answered by reporting to the press and in widely distributed school reports of such data as expenditures per pupil, the school's accreditation, follow-up studies of students in collegiate institutions, success of students in competitive activities, scores on standardized tests, and special projects. Such answers are simplistic, inadequate, and often lack validity. Schools located where parental incomes and aspirations are high, where per pupil expenditures are high, and where community expectations are high tend to show up very well on such comparisons.

But is the school program as good as it should be? If the question is answered, the response is usually that it would be better if the district spent even more money and if the teacher-pupil ratio were even smaller. Again, such answers lack adequate evidence to support the claims. The positive approach is to collect a variety of data with subsequent analyses in the pattern that the school design here suggests.

The *school for everyone* pays more attention than do conventional schools to the nature of reports, who receives them, who is affected by them, and what actions are expected. Above all, the reports are not simply filed—except a copy for historical purposes. If a report does not suggest and help to create action, it has little value except for some historian.

Certainly the most centrally concerned persons should receive reports: parents, students, and professional workers at the building level. Equally important, the reports should indicate what responses are expected and what steps are being taken by the preparers of the reports to see that something happens. Of course, reports should also go from each school to the board of education, superintendent of schools, advisory groups, newspapers, and to other mass media, with comments.

Bad news is as important as good news when the report indicates diagnoses of the situation, prescriptive actions being considered, what implementations are possible, and how future evaluations will be made.

These school reports with the kinds of program evaluation indicated here become live, working tools that impact not only on the people who produce them but on those who are affected by them directly or by implication. Program evaluations that call for responses generate faith that suggestions receive more than passive attention. Increased time and money spent in this process can be extremely productive.

What really happens is that this school is establishing more specific priorities and procedures for continuous improvements. Part 4 of this book provides suggestions to facilitate the change process.

Some Possible First Steps
for School Persons

1. Having considered all six kinds of program evaluation and recognizing the high priorities of steps 1 and 4, decide which of these two—or even parts of them—that you can handle now (consensus of students, teachers, and S-M team). Define your goals in performance teams and select your items in relation to them.

2. Collect and use the data for diagnoses by the three groups, asking each to discuss and reach consensus on prescriptive actions that they believe are possible, how to implement the recommendations, and what further evaluative data to collect and analyze.

3. Present the data and recommendations for discussions and appropriate responses by concerned persons outside the school, of course, with special attention to those persons who exercise external controls but also to inform others via mass media and meetings.

4. Remembering the ultimate necessity of total, basic changes and the interrelationships of all program aspects, recognize the limitations of partial steps and plan ahead on the basis of priorities. Make these decisions a matter of public record with reasons for the delays in actions on items with lower priority.

5. If you have selected the alternative of having a representative group of students working totally or nearly so

on the program of a school for *everyone* that this book describes, use *all* the evaluation techniques with *them*. Also use as many of the techniques as you believe possible, especially Numbers 1 and 4, with the balance of the school, for comparative purposes.

For Parents and Others

1. Your contributions are indicated above in items 1, 3, 5. Ask school employees to suggest materials that you can use to prepare yourselves better for joining with them in analyzing data, looking toward further improvements in the school program.

2. As you read and hear criticisms of educational programs generally or the local school, ask yourself and others such questions as the following in order to arrive at constructive approaches to further improvements:

   a) Who are the critics and what are their motives?

   b) How reliable and valid are the data they present?

   c) Are their prescriptions based on careful diagnoses?

   d) How do they propose to evaluate the program changes they suggest?

Priorities and Procedures

Changing any school may be complicated. However, ways exist to facilitate the process. Systematically planned options help to resolve differences of opinions about *open* and *closed* schools, thus facilitating the process of change. Decisions to implement selected aspects of individualized methods of learning, teaching, and management are less traumatic when everyone has more choices available. Also, the procedures recommended here call for spending money differently rather than to spend more, a goal that usually is popular and unique. Since this school's program involves more persons both inside and outside the premises in plans and operations, there is more widespread understanding of the changes and what happens. Transitional steps that harmonize with the ultimate goals help to make program developments easier and more readily acceptable.

15
Open and Closed Schools

How does clarification of terms and concepts help the process of change? What are the differences between closed and open schools? Which type requires more structure? How may options in schools resolve the differences?

WHY should schools change? Does the need come from pressures to ameliorate some ills in the social order? Or is it because societal pressures force changes in the programs? Schools reflect the social mores in which they exist. The idea that schools may remedy societal ills and produce utopia is attractive. However, that notion is unreal and without precedent.

The realistic aim is to provide students, teachers, and administrators with motivations, rationales, and methods to work with themselves and with others to improve their school. The methodology includes enlightened, constructive criticism, and participatory democratic actions. The focus is on the diagnostic and evaluative efforts that schools practice everyday.

Thus the emphases in this chapter and the balance of Part 4 are on positive programs and actions to change schools. The aim is to indicate some steps that schools might consider in moving from current practices to more desirable ones. Any negativism here is deliberate to show the need for changing those present practices.

Selecting priorities and making decisions about ameliorative procedures are extremely important. This chapter considers the educational environment. Subsequent ones deal with methods of teaching and learning, expenditures of school funds, how to select priorities, relations with the world outside the school building, and the methodology of decision making.

The School Environment

A basic need in planning for change is to understand and define the *present* and the *ultimate* school environments. Every school operates somewhere between a completely closed environment and a completely open one. In reality, there is probably no school at either extreme: open or closed in all aspects of program and personnel operations. What confuses is that some schools that claim to be open are in fact quite closed. The opposite also is true.

A *closed* school environment has conventional classrooms, each with a teacher in charge. It also has class periods of standard length in all subjects except for laboratory sessions which have additional time. One half or more of the subjects that count for graduation are required of everyone. Students work in classrooms, study halls, or libraries, almost always in the school building or on the grounds outside. Homework is assigned quite uniformly. Progress is measured by a five-letter marking system: half or more of the students will receive Cs, about 10 percent As or Fs, and the balance Bs and Ds equally divided.

196

All teachers and students do about the same things, especially in the academic areas. A general attitude prevails that the academic subjects are considerably more important than the so-called non-academic subjects of fine arts, practical arts, and physical education.

At the opposite extreme, the *open* school provides a variety of spaces for teaching and learning, each having dimensions and furnishings related to the specific activities that occur in the space. Homes and the community are used systematically as teaching and learning environments.

The open school has relatively few curriculum requirements for everyone. Standard lengths of time for completing courses do not exist. Courses are included more on the basis of how they help students in the present world in and outside the school and less on the basis of meeting uncertain future needs. Learning is measured more in performance terms than as memorized content. Evaluation in the open school emphasizes changes in individual performance more than comparisons of individuals. The open school in harmony with the times uses more audiovisual aids to learning, with somewhat less emphasis upon reading requirements but certainly not neglecting them. Decisions are based more on what individual students need at a given time.

The open school provides a larger instructional staff, some of whom do not have conventional teaching certificates based on completion of specified college subjects. Students have many opportunities to select their own teachers. A minimum of regularly scheduled group meetings leaves more time for students to study and work individually or with selected groups in the school and community. In all this, the school reflects the philosophy that significant differences exist among individual students and teachers and that they vary considerably at different times.

Schools need not be completely open or completely closed. Forcing all students and all teachers into the same open or closed environment is neither democratic nor humane. To serve the varying needs of every student and teacher requires what both the open and closed environments can provide—a variety of teaching and learning situations with constant, constructive supervision of all personnel. Acceptance of that point of view makes the change process easier because the entire school does not operate on one philosophy or the other.

Personal Relationships

Open schools involve different concepts of adult-student relationships. Possibly the most adverse criticism against the self-contained classroom is that the student is limited for a semester or a year to one teacher, a situation which may not be good for the teacher either. Spending five hours a day in self-contained classrooms also isolates the teacher from the stimulation that comes from working with other teachers and with members of the community.

Students in self-contained classrooms typically have limited opportunities to interact with other students. Most of their time is spent in interacting with the teacher, responding to questions, and following directions. That setting provides minimal experiences for them to work actively with other students on projects or while learning the subject requirements.

A school that is open physically and philosophically deals constructively with these situations. Students work with other students and with a variety of teachers. Even the one-to-one relationship between a student and a teacher adviser can be changed by either party as described in Chapter 3. Teachers work with a variety of students and with other teachers on a more personal basis. Persons outside the school assist teachers and students, thus providing other types of relationships.

These opportunities for expanded human relationships, however, must not be taken for granted. Cliques may form in open schools as easily as in others. Teacher advisers and others need to conduct sociometric investigations from time to time to discover who works with whom, on what occasions, and with what satisfactions and difficulties. These data also help to develop readiness for change.

Certainly there are some students who need constant interaction on a temporary basis with one teacher. Also, groupings of students for a time are appropriate for a variety of reasons. However, decisions on these matters result from professional prescriptions after diagnosis and not merely for the convenience of teachers or school administrators.

Curriculum and Time

The conventional school curriculum organization is simple. There are subjects called United States history, tenth grade English, typing or public speaking. Some schools have different levels of courses, such as basic or general, industrial or commercial, or college preparatory. Some of these subjects are required; others are elected. Once a student decides to take one of these courses, usually a semester or a year must be spent in that course; moreover, there have to be enough students to elect a course before it can be taught.

The "mini-courses," becoming increasingly common, often have definite time requirements for everyone. That situation still is relatively closed. However, such developments provide transitions to an open school where students may take courses of varied degrees of difficulty, for different lengths of time, and start them almost at any time with an adviser's approval. That goal requires more organization and of a different nature than does the conventional program in which the teacher knows that the students are going to be there for a stated length of time.

Fortunately, schools now may keep track of individual student's progress through the use of computer programs.

Printouts show their advisers and other interested persons where the students are and what they have accomplished. The process of change is easier because teachers and administrators have better information.

Evaluation and Personnel Policies

The conventional school evaluates pupil progress with a relatively closed system of letter grades. A student's achievements on tests, class discussion, papers, and special projects are averaged—sometimes adjusted up or down to reward effort or punish behavior—to give periodic grades or final grades in various courses. Those marks determine rank-in-class, admission to a university, and often employment. The organization of that system is quite simple.

Individualized appraisal and reporting of pupil progress is more complex. Everything a student does is important. As shown in Chapter 13, the method is to record the number of segments that a student completes in the learning sequence in the major areas of human knowledge, as well as the unique or special things that a student does. Also recorded are the student's scores on standardized measuring instruments, both norm-based and criterion-referenced, to provide a basis of comparison between this student and others.

A productive transitional step from conventional practices to the evaluation system of pupil progress in the *school for everyone* is to supplement the single letter grade with a report and a record of the unique things each student does, as described in Chapter 13. The extra time spent in writing these brief reports will be productive both in good will and in motivation for improved work.

The open school's supervisory-management team recognizes the differences among individuals in talents, interests, and preparation, so that each person does what he or she is most able to do. This arrangement calls for more separation of functions, along with an organization to avoid duplication and assure coordination. Precisely the same analogy applies to the "all-purpose" teacher *vis-a-vis* the concept of differentiated staffing as presented in Chapter 4. The compensatory advantages to staff members were pointed out in those earlier chapters.

Transitional steps for teachers include scheduling two or more teachers with the support of clerical, instructional, and general aides as described in Chapter 4, and a group of students, for a block of time—the more of each the better, all depending on local decisions by the persons involved. Similarly, the differentiated staff for supervision and management may be started for a part of the school or to introduce some aspects of the program in Chapter 5.

Openness without increased planning, structural analyses, and specific assignments and goals produces chaos. Many of today's conventional schools with loosely defined purposes and practices, in a relatively unstructured and at times unsystematic manner, fail to produce the kinds of services to persons, to curriculum, and to all the other aspects of schooling that are needed if tomorrow's schools are to be better than today's. On the other hand, an unplanned open school will not achieve its goals either. That is why this chapter emphasizes transitional procedures in relation to established priorities.

The Role of Options in Changing Schools

This philosophy of school organization and management that emphasizes alternatives facilitates the process of change from conventional arrangements to the *school for everyone*. Since a school should not be completely open or closed, the transition wisely provides a variety of programs. Students and teachers make choices; the supervisory management team provides the arrangements and sees to it that the programs work well.

A reasonable start would include one part of the school, where the teachers, supervisors, and students function as prescribed in this book. Another part would be completely conventional with most subjects required—those being mainly academic, school bound except for homework assignments, and with self-contained classrooms, the ABCDF grading system, and the like. A third part of the school would resemble what most schools are like today: transitional in nature between the two foregoing plans. Larger schools might have several transitional schools, each with unique characteristics.

The change process thus described must be accompanied by the collection of data to help everyone understand what is happening to students and teachers and how productive they are in the various schools within the total program. What really is occurring is that alternatives are *open* to everyone in all aspects of the program. The school respects diversity among its clients, its employees, and the communities it serves.

These differences among locales—and even within a given school and in separate aspects of its program—may cause consternation among persons who deplore the limited use of comparative research data in education. Such criticism is not well-founded. The necessary data come from studies of one time in relation to another in the same school locale.

Options do not require separate schools, segregated staffs and students, or dichotomous policies that produce an either-or philosophy. The school organization described here has alternative provisions, under positive controls to meet everyone's changing needs. The school is not merely permissive; it has a structured approach to assure options. That goal requires prodigious planning but holds enormous hope.

The following chapters provide more details. The emphasis is on how-to-do-it. A reminder at this point is important to the practical teacher or administrator: everything does not have to be done at once nor is the same program followed by all persons in the school. The method is to provide more options.

Some Possible First Steps
for School Persons

1. Discuss some aspect of school management in order to bring out changes in methodology that will make the school more *open* or *closed*.

2. Take the same aspect and develop a set of procedures that any teacher in any conventional classroom could utilize to make the program there more individualized.

3. As a student with a particular option that you wish you had available, submit a proposal for a change in your program to the appropriate person in your school. Be specific in such matters as what you want to do, how you propose to do it, where and for how long, and how the results are to be evaluated.

For Parents and Others

1. Since expressions of some persons and media presentations show confusion about the term, "open education," ask school persons to organize a study group to consider changes in school structures that would permit more individualization with increased total productivity for the school program. The goal would be increased enlightenment to offset the heated arguments that sometimes result from inaccurate proposals and reports.

16

Teaching and Learning

What forces influence schools? How are decisions made to try new ideas or different programs? How does the school for everyone resolve problems with more options for students, teachers, and the supervisory-management team? Who is in charge of whom?

WHO decides whether or not to try new methods and programs? The answer is complex, varying from place to place. Teachers and/or students offer suggestions, as do others. In many schools, the principal makes the decision to change. In others the decision-making power is with central office personnel.

Local boards of education and superintendents with their central office staffs issue policy statements and prescriptions. In larger cities, these directions also can be relatively remote from a local school, even when area offices are created to bridge the gap.

Legally, schools are creatures of the states. Their control over educational programs, however, are remote, mostly tied to finance. State departments of education often encourage innovative practices in schools by providing funds marked for designated programs. Private foundations exercise influence by granting funds for specified developments. Aggressive salespersons, commercial groups, pressure groups, and others urge changes in methods, materials, and programs.

In the final analysis, the decision to seek better teaching and learning is mainly local, school by school, by the persons who work there—with approval of their governing bodies. This decentralized approach has produced changes and continues to encourage the search for better ways to conduct teaching and learning.

The Past Has Produced Changes

This concept of a *school for everyone* is neither new nor unique. No conventional school today allows students nearly as much time for independent study as did the one-room school. Few schools today make as effective use of the community as a learning environment as vocational agriculture programs did more than a half century ago—and still do. Those were the days when a youngster could enter the first grade not by the date of birth but at the decision of the teacher with the mother. The continuous progress concept, although done quite poorly years ago, was called double-promotion.

Were schools better a half-century or more ago than they are today? The answer depends upon the criteria that persons use. Those schools had shortcomings that do not exist today even in conventional schools. On the other hand, in the zeal for efficiency and improved teaching and administration, some features of individualization that characterized schools then have since been abandoned.

World War II interrupted the progress toward more individualized learning and professionalized teaching undertaken during the educationally exciting decade of the 1930s. Physical education, global geography, and industrial education received considerable emphasis in the interests of winning the war.

National defense programs in the 1950s and early 1960s emphasized the fields of mathematics, science, and foreign language with greatly increased numbers of school counselors to urge large student enrollments in these fields. Some good was done, but many students were turned off by the resultant programs. During the same period, foundations and governments supported a variety of programs aimed to individualize learning in schools, to make better use of television and other news media, and to obtain better utilization of the professional talents of teachers.

Extensive national projects in English and social studies reshuffled the curriculum and modernized teaching in these fields but failed to make the kinds of curriculum decisions described in Chapter 6. Efforts to improve the fine arts usually focused on excellence and appreciation rather than on how to utilize the ideas of form, beauty, and culture in all aspects of living for all persons.

Advances in data processing seemed to offer potential for individualizing school programs, but unfortunately those techniques were most often used to do faster what should not be done anyway. They printed out the same kinds of grading and reporting forms. Modular schedules changed time allocations but little else. Better records of expenditures for school supplies, equipment, and personnel seldom changed the philosophy of the schools in making better uses of them.

Many of these innovations of the fifties and sixties were fragmentary and disappeared soon after the money to stimulate them was gone. These efforts, however, contributed to the present dissatisfactions with the status quo and produced readiness for change. Relatively few persons want to return to a particular kind of school in the past—even though they have difficulties in arriving at consensus about what needs to be done.

Examining Some Key Issues

Barriers to school improvement arise when people spend too much time and energy in defending their opinions instead of seeking better solutions and more workable programs.

Almost two decades ago, this author identified and discussed "Eighteen Representative Issues to be Resolved" if education were to improve. They are included here because they represent examples of the need for resolution, not for defending positions at one extreme or the other as is done so frequently.

Discussing these issues *now* can enable you and others to take significant first steps in developing the options that *a school for everyone* needs:

1. *Freedom and Compulsion* —Whether educational programs of the future shall develop students who feel free to conform or to rebel constructively, and who understand how to participate in moderate social action—or whether they shall produce students with a compulsion to conform or to rebel and who either assume a laissez-faire attitude or conduct violent social action.

2. *Communication* —Whether the school shall develop students who communicate effectively with their peers—or shall continue to produce those who fail to listen, observe, speak, or write well.

3. *Independent Judgment* — Whether the school shall plan programs to help students know when to rely on their own judgment and resources—or shall allow them to depend on some adult or other person to whom they are personally attracted for some reason or other.

4. *Using Knowledge* —Whether the school program shall develop students who understand that knowledge is essential for creativity or inquiry—or shall encourage students to ignore basic knowledge, or value it largely for its own sake.

5. *Men and Machines* —Whether teachers shall resolve for themselves and their students the respective roles of men and machines—or shall ridicule or ignore technical progress.

6. *Explaining and Discovering* —Whether teachers shall make enlightened choices between explaining matters to students and encouraging students to discover things for themselves—or whether they shall over-emphasize one or the other in their teaching.

7. *Professionalizing Teaching* —Whether teachers as individuals or in their organizations shall work for institutional arrangements that can professionalize teaching— or shall continue to focus narrowly on certain salary, welfare, and certification aspects of a job.

8. *Curriculum Organization* —Whether the school shall develop curricula that are logically and sequentially planned from the beginning to the end of organized education—or shall continue a pattern of artificial divisions, unnecessary or unplanned repetitiveness, and arbitrary terminal arrangements.

9. *Basic and Depth Education* —Whether institutional arrangements shall reduce or eliminate the competition among subjects for the basic education time of students and yet provide time for specialized interests—or shall continue to encourage curricular competitiveness and inbalances.

10. *Independent Study* —Whether schools shall create settings that encourage independent study by pupils and professional activities for teachers—or shall continue to

foster conditions that inhibit those objectives through rigid use of space, time, numbers, and content.

11. *National and Local Control*—Whether schools shall decide what curricular and other educational arrangements need national uniformity and what need the imprint of local and regional differences—or shall control these matters locally as much as possible.

12. *Student Grouping*—Whether schools shall vary the size and composition of pupil groups with the purposes and content of instruction and the needs of individual students—or shall continue to use standard-sized classes and classrooms for all purposes.

13. *Appraising and Reporting Student Progress*—Whether schools shall carefully record the progress of each student in all aspects of learning that the school monitors, noting especially the particular productivity of each student in comparison to his or her own previous efforts, while using norm-based instruments to help the student assess better his or her talents and accomplishments—or shall schools continue to compare students with other students of a particular group with resultant grades of A B C D F, or pass-fail, and the preparation of reports showing rank in the particular class or group to which the student belongs.

14. *Human Resources*—Whether the school shall constantly reevaluate the use of human resources—or whether it shall follow conventional policies that emphasize uniformity, standardization, and operational smoothness.

15. *Educational Facilities*—Whether schools shall develop rational educational specifications and then build and remodel accordingly—or shall permit routine material features or standard designs to get in the way of sound educational practices.

16. *School Money* —Whether schools shall spend relatively less money for some aspects of instructional services and capital outlay and more for others, the criterion being quality or educational outcomes—or shall continue to follow standardized fiscal policies that tend to ignore relationships between financial input and product output.

17. *Evaluation* —Whether schools shall evaluate school excellence on standards that are essentially qualitative—or shall continue to use those that are mainly quantitative.

18. *Professionalizing Supervision and Management* — Whether individuals engaged in supervision and management will have assignments especially related to each one's talents and interests with a staff broad enough to cover the various functions that need to be done—or shall continue to assume that all members engaged in supervision and management will have the same kind of training and be expected to be expert in all aspects of the tasks.

The question is not which point of view is right but rather how may a school accommodate divergent points of view? The challenge is to provide as many alternatives as possible and reasonable with continuous evaluations to help everyone make better decisions about teaching, learning, and supervising.

Program Planning and Decision Making

A basic characteristic of this school is that everyone has a voice in decisions that can influence personal achievements or the school program. That goal contrasts with conventional situations where sociometric analyses reveal the importance of knowing *whom* to talk to about *what* is needed in order to get something done. Direct communication among students, parents, teacher advisers, counselors, and the principal or assistant principal provides the action when any one of them requires attention in scheduling, locus of study and work, progress or lack of it, and a host of other important considerations.

Whom do you see to get action on such-and-such a personal concern, a program change, to have a repair made, or some new supplies or equipment? The key to answering those questions and others is in the differentiated staffing arrangements with the specified lines of authority and decision making as described in Chapters 3, 4, and 5, along with the comprehensive program evaluation methods proposed in Chapter 14.

Structure without substance, however, is inadequate. Conventional schools have formal and informal ways to get things done. Many persons in them have learned how to play the games in those relatively closed environments. Analyses reveal the devious routes. The difficulty is that some persons are more successful than others, a factor that is not conducive to high morale and equality of opportunities.

The decision-making process and the necessary communication lines must be equally open to all regardless of status. The voice of the least powerful student, teacher, or supervisor-manager needs to be heard and acted upon the same as any other. The teacher adviser system and the supervisory-management arrangements described in this book make that goal possible.

Decision making also is widely shared. The more open the school, the greater the opportunities for that result to occur. Periodic investigations, trial efforts, and continuous evaluations ensure that it does.

Many of today's practices are contrary to the foregoing goals. The situation results from collective bargaining, strikes, grievance procedures, negotiations, and the like which seem necessary because individuals believe they are not allowed to participate adequately in making decisions. Breakdowns in communication and the reluctance of governing bodies to act in the spirit of the proposals constitute other barriers.

These breakdowns result from a variety of causes. Completely opposite points of view, unwillingness of some individuals to talk with others, issues that have highly explosive inherent qualities, unreasonable selfishness, and attempts to make decisions about matters over which persons have no legal control are only a few examples.

Human selfishness and other aspects of nature are not changed in a weekend or a month. On the other hand, as persons in more open schools, in homes, and in community environments experience cooperative give-and-take and consensus-reaching approaches to decision making, the results can be much better than conventionally is the case.

Most strikes and grievance procedures result from the unwillingness of persons to reach reasonable consensus. Ultimately they do so but in the meantime, schools close, tempers flare, violence develops, and other occurences result from yes or no answers that interfere with operations and human rights. Sometimes, of course, students, teachers, parents, administrators, and others do not know or accept their rights and responsibilities. Ultimately judges and juries may have to make decisions instead of the school people themselves. That outcome is not the goal we seek.

What are the answers?

The *priority* in this school for everyone, as reiterated time and again, is for optional programs of personalization. The antithesis is when a conventional school applies policies equally to everyone. The *procedures* here in Part 4 emphasize the development of unique goals for a given institution and for each individual related to it. The fewer "yes or no" answers the better. The task of each person who has to help someone else make a decision is to consider the available alternatives and to select the best one, recognizing that further decisions down the road are possible.

Uniformity and Variety

Variety is said to be the spice of life. That is true for many persons. Other individuals find more satisfaction in uniformity. Moreover, individuals change their perceptions from time to time. The school that adopts uniform policies and programs for all students, teachers, and the supervisory-management team cannot possibly help every person to develop human potential to the fullest.

Providing options makes the operation of a school a simpler process. A school that adopts and forces uniform policies and procedures on everyone brings unnecessary problems to those persons who are responsible for managing the enterprise. For example, to announce a policy that no one in the school will receive a failing grade is just as wrong as it would be to say that the possibility of receiving a failing grade is inflicted upon everyone.

No defensible reason exists for forcing all students into any system. There are sound reasons for the proposals in Chapter 13 for evaluating pupil progress. True professionals will consider and explain the viable alternatives suggested there.

The fetish of uniformity that characterizes so many educational programs develops from the false notion that such procedures are the fairest way to treat all individuals. More realistically, such policies develop so that administrators do not have to think so much about what is best for the individuals who are concerned.

Supervising and managing an enterprise that seeks to develop fully the interests and talents of each individual calls for a methodology that has not been emphasized adequately in most preparation programs for teachers and administrators. There never has been, nor can there ever be, a single best way to organize the curriculum, to design a school building and provide supplies and equipment in it, or to prepare teachers to teach, to organize learning and evaluate progress. That is why options are essential.

Chaos Is Not the Outcome

Alternative decisions about teaching and learning need not produce confusion and disorder. All the alternatives are under control and supervision.

Someone is always observing and evaluating the results: teachers and teacher advisers over students, supervisor-managers over the differentiated instructional staffs, central office personnel over the local school supervisory-management team, officials in state education departments and regional accrediting associations over all the others, and the public over everyone—and conversely in all cases.

How decisions are made is one key issue. How the outcomes are evaluated is another. The goal is constantly to make the school a better institution for everyone. Systematic decision making with constant attention and follow-up enhances human values. Somebody cares!

The alternative approaches urged in this chapter make changing a school an easier and more effective process. One question remaining is, will it cost more in taxes or personal expenses? The chapter that follows this one provides answers.

Some Possible First Steps
for School Persons

1. Think of the most recent controversy in your school or an attack on the program as it now exists. Then through processes of involvement by personal contacts or mail, find the variety of proposed solutions that persons have to suggest. Be sure to involve some parents and other taxpayers, as well as the staff and students.

2. Select several of the proposed solutions—based both on frequency and ease of implementation —that will likely find wide acceptance.

3. Provide these options in a well developed and evaluated program.

For Parents and Others

1. Perhaps you have harbored in your mind for some time an adverse criticism of present school programs. Think how the school could meet your objections without forcing your ideas on everyone. What options do you propose? Then discuss your ideas on that basis with school officials, using the approaches described in this chapter.

17
Costs and Productivity

What methods are best for assuring accountability in school programs? How can the performance of students, teachers, and supervisor-managers be improved? How are expenditures related to productivity?

HOW a school district spends its money actually reflects the educational philosophy of the voters, the governing body, and the employees. That generalization applies to all districts regardless of the finances available.

The basic question that school employees and other related officials need to answer is: what changes in outcomes for students, teachers, supervisor-managers, and the community in general result from past, present, or proposed financial expenditures? Stated differently, how does financial input affect product output?

Answers to such questions do not come easily for a number of reasons. Some procedures are beyond the control of school personnel. Powerful pressure groups influence the passage of laws and enforcement of regulations. Also, there are sudden and at times unexpected changes in what money buys, effects of supply and demand on personnel and goods, unanticipated alterations in school needs, policies, and outcomes, and others.

Confusions About Causes and Effects

School districts vary widely in the amount of available funds to support schools. The affluent ones can and usually do pay higher salaries to their employees, spend more funds on supplies and equipment, provide more services, have lower teacher-pupil ratios, build more expensive school structures, have more books in libraries with more elaborate facilities to house them, and furnish more services than do other less affluent school districts. These superior finances usually result from higher tax bases produced by industry, business, luxurious residential areas, or other special resources.

The pupils in these affluent school districts come from higher income homes where the parents believe in the kind of education that the school provides and the kind of expenditures that the program represents. Most of the parents are college graduates who have high expectations of their children. The parents are also capable and willing to help their sons and daughters.

Consequently, the pupils from these homes do relatively well on standardized tests and other norm-based examinations. More of them go on to colleges and universities and more of them succeed then do students from average or below average income homes. The natural assumption, therefore, is that quality education results from the expenditure of more money per capita.

Conversely, in areas that are not so affluent, teachers' salaries may be lower, fewer books are in the library, and the building may be old and shabby. Moreover, the students who graduate from these schools do not go in large numbers to universities; certainly not so many of them go to the prestigious ones. The students do not perform as well on standardized and norm-based examinations nor do they win as many academic awards as their counterparts in more affluent areas.

The conclusion is that the school system does not spend enough money and that the whole situation would be reversed if the expenditures were increased substantially. Is that logic sound?

The idea that school quality depends directly upon the amount of money spent per pupil has produced some shocking results in recent times. Many people conclude that if the amount of money spent on inner-city or rural youth were increased to the levels of the affluent suburban areas, the quality of education would be increased. The results are disappointing. It simply does not work that way.

Costs of This School Design

The *school for everyone* described here does not need to spend more money than conventional schools, except possibly for some initial expenditures. For example, it may be necessary to spend money to help parents and taxpayers understand what increased individualization and the redeployment of the professional staff really mean.

Such money would be well spent—especially when one considers that money has been spent improperly in some communities to provide parents and taxpayers with erroneous concepts: the need to reduce class size, to increase teacher salaries, to consolidate districts, to construct new buildings, and to purchase expensive supplies and equipment as sure ways to improve teaching and learning.

Truly professional people—as long as they have proper support staffs—should be paid salaries that compare favorably with those paid to other persons with similar university preparation and with comparable responsibilities. As the school described here produces better outcomes for students and the homes and the community it serves, the reasons for higher salaries for the teachers and administrators who make it work become increasingly apparent.

The emphasis here is on spending money differently. School costs can and must be related directly to productivity as shown later in this chapter.

Costs and Program Characteristics

The need increasingly is to show how different school expenditures may increase student and staff productivity. Such analyses give the people who provide financial support and other types of assistance confidence that their efforts to change programs and expenditures are producing better results. The paragraphs that follow show how this can be done.

Chapter 3 emphasized the role and the contributions of the teacher adviser system. If one assumes that teachers have a work week of approximately 40 hours, the suggested allocation of five hours a week to the function of teacher adviser calls for the expenditure of one-eighth of the average teacher's salary for this activity. The statistic here involves a relationship to the total salaries of all teachers in the school rather than in terms of what is paid to a given individual.

The following questions illustrate how a school can measure the productivity of this expenditure:

- To what extent has each student in the school arrived at tentative career choice(s) and developed a series of hobbies or special interests?

- What effect has the program had on numbers and characteristics of dropouts and failures, both of which the teacher-adviser system aims to decrease sharply?

- How have the self-images of students in this school changed?

- Whom do students see now in order to solve a problem, resolve some dilemma or make some decision that is important to the individual? What are the outcomes?

If the answers to these questions and others that the staff and community list are more positive than the answers provided in the past, the taxpayers have a basis for knowing that the expenditures of funds along these lines is more productive in this school than formerly.

Chapter 4 presented the picture of a school where teaching was more truly a profession. How does the performance of teachers in this school differ now from what teachers did formerly and what are the results? Here are questions that need answers with significant data:

- What curriculum changes have occurred?

- Is there more precise evaluation of pupil progress?

- Is there increased use of community resources?

- What different teaching materials has the staff developed?

- Do teachers spend less time on clerical duties?

- Have teachers been released for more productive work through the help of instructional assistants?

- What new materials, professional articles, new methods, and the like, have teachers produced?

- Have teachers found and are teachers using their own special interests and performance in areas where they have special talents—again as compared with teachers in this school in the past?

- How much time do teachers spend with individual students as contrasted with groups of students?

Chapter 5 discussed what the supervisory-management team needs to do. Many of the same questions that were raised with respect to teachers are relevant here for the collection of data on productivity as compared with base-line data in this school. Specific answers to such questions as the following are analyzed:

- How much time do the principal and assistant principal spend directly in working with teachers and what activities are used to improve the quality of teaching and learning?

- What is the quantity and quality of information about the school that the external relations director provides?

- What evidence shows that the community has better information than formerly about school expenditures, services to students with special problems, relationships with other community agencies, employers, school activities, and the like, and the productivity of the differentiated staff for supervision and management?

The answers to the foregoing questions about changes in performance of persons are essential for determining whether taxpayers, parents, and students are getting increased productivity for the dollars they invest.

Chapter 6 described a school program in which fundamental and productive curriculum revisions occur. The analyses in relation to costs consider what has happened.

- To what extent has the school reduced the amount and kinds of content and activities defined as essential and, therefore required of all students?

- Are students less bored with school than they formerly were?

- How many students believe that the curriculum in the school is relevant to their needs and interests?

- What changes have occurred in hobby and career choices by individual students?

Chapter 7 analyzed where learning occurs and how to choose the best locale for it to happen. The analysis of productivity examines changes in homework and how the community is utilized as a learning environment.

- How much time proportionately do students spend in learning activities in the three locales—school, home, and community?

- What learning outcomes happen in each of the three places?

- How have school expenditures changed as a result of systematic use of the community and homes as learning centers?

Chapter 8 described methods used for motivating students, teachers, and the supervisory-management team. Numerous questions were posed in this chapter about how people spend their time and with what productivity. The emphasis was on comparisons of a school at one time *vis-a-vis* a later time with analyses extending over a number of years in such outcomes as the following:

- How has the school's program for motivating students, teachers, and members of the supervisory-management team increased their productivity?

- Do they feel more satisfied?

Chapter 9 emphasized the development of human relations and interactional skills. The productivity measures here concern how people are getting along in the various environments:

- Do sociometric measures indicate more and different kinds of contacts by students with each other and with adults as compared with those contacts previously?

- What comparable changes do teachers and supervisors experience?

Chapter 10 developed the concept of study and work. Since these aspects represent the heart of the learning process, productivity concerns learning the essentials, doing special projects and creative activities, as well as scores on various types of tests. The data need to indicate:

- What do various kinds of students do that is not required?

- How does this productivity compare with the required-and-elective system that operated previously?

- How does student learning in homes and in the community now compare with earlier homework and the use of community resources?

Chapter 11 concerned the elements of time, number, money, spaces, and educational supplies and equipment. The data are:

- How do all of these structural elements in the school compare with or contrast in quantity and effectiveness with similar data from earlier times?

Chapter 12 dealt with the appearance of the school. Productivity is related to how well the building and grounds serve the needs of the educational program.

- Do the facilities produce negative, neutral, or positive effects, as revealed by judgment on a checklist?

- How does the extent of duplicated facilities among school, homes, community compare with data from earlier studies?

Chapter 13 dealt with evaluating and reporting pupil progress. The productivity study analyzes the quantity and quality of information that students, parents, employers, and colleges receive in comparison to the A B C D F or similar marking system the school used previously:

- How does the new information compare in quantity and quality with letter grades?

- Since this activity represents one of the most important functions that a school performs, how much more time, effort, and money is given to evaluating and reporting pupil progress as contrasted with earlier analyses?

Chapter 14 outlined the methods of evaluating the program. Data are collected to answer these questions:

- Do more people understand better and believe more in the program?

- What changes on norm-based or criterion-referenced measuring devices have occurred since the previous evaluation?

- How does the productivity of this school compare in all aspects with similar studies done earlier?

These Data Are Crucial

What may appear as redudancy in this chapter is deliberate. The basic questions are: Should a school district spend increased funds on a conventional school? Should affluent communities that spend money easily and express satisfaction with what its favored students produce really feel satisfied with their productivity?

The reader will notice that the comparisons of data are with those findings in the *same* school at an earlier date rather than with some other school. The usual approaches are otherwise. That temptation must be resisted because of environmental differences that influence and contaminate the results. Are *we* as good as *they*? is a natural question. The answers may motivate changes. However, the opposite effect also is possible: We can never be as good as they.

This writer believes that any nation, state, city, or county must use a method that analyzes increases in productivity from year to year *within* the same school environment rather than emphasize comparisons *between* one school and another. The concept here is that any school may produce better results with present resources. A basic step is to do better with what you have.

The analyses presented in this chapter call for different methods and more efforts in evaluation than most schools provide. However, these steps constitute the only defensible way of measuring whether a school is actually performing as well as it should be doing. Even more important, are increased expenditures for whatever purpose producing better results for students, teachers, or supervisor-managers?

Increased expenditures to cover increased costs of living and raw materials are one thing. Increases for improved productivity are quite another. The *school for everyone* serves both needs as costs and results are related.

The data must provide analyses that everyone can understand. Equally important, the people that receive the reports must have motivations and the methods to do something constructively. For example, if students have not developed identifiable and recorded hobbies or special interests beyond the school's required curriculum, the teacher adviser system is not working. The total number of students with these shortcomings indicates degrees of the system's successes or failures.

Then there must be a careful diagnosis, including analyses of comprehensive data, to produce one or more prescriptions for further improvements in the system, as described in Chapter 5. After a period of implementation — putting decisions into practice — the results are analyzed again to show improvements or the need for further changes. The same procedures are used with *every ques-*

tion listed earlier in this chapter—as well as other questions that school and community persons evolve.

There is no other way for taxpayers outside the school and persons in it to get better results from the money they spend. That commitment brings a sharp break from expectations and actions in conventional schools and in some recent state programs for improving so-called accountability.

Responsibility for relating costs to production rests primarily with the persons involved with the activity. Teachers need to analyze how they spend their time and what results come from what they cost the taxpayers. Students and teachers should analyze time, materials, and programs. Supervisors and managers should do the same for their own activities and help students and teachers in their responsibilities as indicated.

Central office persons can help to develop procedures and materials to assist local school persons in these processes—as well as analyze their own efforts. The board of education needs to adopt policies that require these studies, reports, and recommendations—and then develop further policies to improve the situations.

All of these responsibilities and efforts are directed not toward blind economies or petty motives but rather to achieve better satisfactions and productivity for everyone. Schooling can be more effective and efficient when the focus is clear and sharp on providing an environment where each individual student, teacher, and other employee has optimum satisfactions and productivity. Those goals are not antithetical as some persons and organizations sometimes say because they have failed to analyze situations scientifically and humanely.

This *school for everyone* takes a positive approach to relating costs and results. To do so requires unconventional approaches to public relations as indicated in the next chapter.

Some Possible First Steps
for School Persons

1. Since the number of questions posed in this chapter may be overwhelming, the suggestion is that you and your colleagues select one or two of the items for investigation. No outside person or one individual can decide effectively for you what items are most crucial in your community.

2. Having decided what to study, be sure to state in measurable terms what performance and productivity are expected. Then collect the data, noting the present costs of producing the results you have achieved. Keep the resultant data for future comparisons.

3. The next step is to make whatever changes in your program that you believe are both possible and important.

4. Repeat Steps 1 and 2 after the new program has operated for a length of time, in most cases for a year at least. Compare the data with what the former program produced. Then analyze what has or has not produced differences in your findings so that you may diagnose the results for possible further prescriptive actions.

For Parents and Other Persons

1. Some taxpayers' organizations appear to have only one interest—to reduce taxes—without reference to effects on school productivity. The focus is on school taxes because those costs often are the only ones over which local persons have direct controls. Closer cooperation with school persons in designing studies of more productive procedures is essential. The first step is to attain better communications with school persons in order to conduct studies of the type that this chapter suggests.

2. Organizations of parents and teachers, that increasingly include students, should take leadership in involving other community persons and groups. The goal is to make democracy really function by seeking consensus and action by the majority of persons rather than by smaller segments of the population, that is, special pressure groups.

18

Relating to the Public

What do conventional programs of public relations accomplish? How do schools create better understanding among persons inside and outside the place of what needs to be done to improve educational programs? What functions do innovative schools provide for boards of education, state departments of education, regional accrediting associations, and universities?

IDEAS about public relations as well as the varied associations and connections within the school that this book advocates differ from those in many conventional schools. What happens here also contrasts markedly with practices that business and industry as well as some governmental agencies and schools follow in their promotional and information releases.

Too often, public relations aims to cover up the bad and exploit the good as the institution or organization defines those two qualities.

The design here complements this "show and tell" with "come join us and see for yourself," in a concept of openness. This school constantly seeks better ways of doing things and relating to people. The goal is not merely to sell a program.

The rationale of some school public relations programs is to protect their staffs from external criticism and in turn to create an image that all is well inside. That kind of advertising aims to create a favorable impression with external groups, seldom involving them to the degree envisioned here in the *school for everyone.*

The constitutencies of any school are extremely complex, touching as they do *all* elements of society. In turn the school itself is an unbelievably complex institution, ever changing, elusive, and difficult for both those within and outside to understand and to cope with adequately. Distrust, antagonisms, and uncertainties are commonplace in spite of the fact that there exists considerable good will on all sides.

Increased youth crime, vandalism, antagonisms, and revolt against conventional moralities produce tremendous misunderstandings that place the school in difficult and sometimes impossible relations with external bodies and persons. Many outsiders expect the schools to do what other persons and agencies have failed to accomplish. When an individual or a gang of young people raid neighborhood establishments, private yards and buildings, or public places, law enforcement agencies often use schools as scapegoats. Proponents of racial equality likewise expect schools to accomplish what others ignore or fail to do. School persons, as a result, become bitter and disillusioned.

The school must have two-way communication between all the persons in it and with all the persons outside. Both groups are composed of diverse persons with greatly varied interests, needs, and ideas. Communication must flow all ways among and between these diverse groups.

Involvement Creates Understanding

This *school for everyone* is closer and more open than others to the homes and the community in which it exists, to the public it serves, and to the board of education responsible for developing, approving, and evaluating the policies under which the school operates. Closeness to the homes comes from more personal involvement and openness on both sides as well as with the provision of better information.

Parents know whom to contact at the school; moreover, a teacher-adviser (as described in Chapter 3) really knows their son or daughter, is concerned, is available, and is *able to do something* when help is needed. Also, the information in expanded analyses and reports of student progress (Chapter 13) provides better information to them. An expanded supervisory-management team, with the more precise allocations of responsibilities that Chapter 5 describes indicates to anyone outside the school whom to appeal to if they do not find satisfactory answers and solutions from the first person they contact.

Not all homes have children in the school. However, the constant search on the part of the school for the help of instructional assistants and for persons in the community who have specialized talents, interests, collections of materials, travel experiences, work experiences, and hobbies brings closer relationships between the schools and the homes or other agencies than a conventional school ever attains. At the same time, these contacts are handled in a way that the individual who does not wish to be involved feels no pressure to do so.

The school program emphasizes not only that the home is one of the three vital learning environments (the other two being the school and the community), but also that the persons in the school have thought seriously about what persons in homes and other environments may contribute. That goal contrasts sharply with the methods of making homework assignments that conventional schools use. There exists a continuous two-way communication between home and school.

Much the same may be said with respect to community involvement. The offices, industrial establishments, agencies, and other community elements find their relations with the school much more open as they are used regularly as resources. This two-way street is as open as possible for both school and community members to travel. Community persons by this process thus understand better what needs to be done in the school *vis-a-vis* at home and in the community.

The whole process of open communications leaves better understandings on the part of taxpayers. As more persons are involved, they know what is going on because they or their friends or acquaintances may have a part in it. This kind of public relations contrasts with the conventional campaigns for raising school taxes which seem to resemble ads for soap or automobiles. Closeness to professional teachers helps to produce better understanding on both sides—provided each one knows what services are needed and how they may provide the help or information required.

The School and Bodies That Control It

Open school staffs have closer relationships with their boards of education than do those in conventional schools, especially where there are several high schools in the same school district. Board members know better what is going on because they have more access to the programs, more than they would know about the conventional school which has relatively closed classrooms.

Conflicts between teachers and boards of education, even those which end in strikes and closed schools, arise for many reasons. Board members under pressure from taxpayers to hold the line against salary increases may have little understanding of what really goes on in the schools. In many conventional schools, respect for the integrity of other persons, based on suspicion rather than open communications, is unduly limited.

Throughout this book the emphasis is on the solution of problems and the development of programs by the methodology of better diagnosis of the causes of difficulties. The open school collects more data, uses more persons in analyzing the data to arrive at prescriptive actions, and involves many persons in implementing and evaluating the results.

Suppose that persons in the neighborhood of the school or even beyond criticize the teachers and administrators because too many students are roaming the streets, committing acts of vandalism, stealing, and other anti-social acts. The traditional school probably hires more guards and emphasizes in news releases what a fine program the school has, highlighting the achievements of outstanding students. The *school for everyone*, on the other hand, takes positive steps to help dissident students to find constructive activities in the school—and when desirable away from the confines of the building—that such persons can accept. Supervision as described elsewhere in this book, with monitoring by the teacher adviser, avoids the syndrome of permissiveness and lack of caring.

Mostly the school program described here is in harmony with the established policies of the board of education. However, if present policies for conventional schools (for example, time schedules, class size, or teacher-pupil ratio) conflict with what the more open school requires, the board members have studied the reasons for differences and made plans accordingly. As a result, they know the reasons for the design, how it operates, and the evaluation of the program. School board members and the professional staff of the school understand and respect each other on a higher professional level in the process.

The policies of the board of education need to recognize the necessity of different educational programs among the high schools of the city or county because of the particular community that each school serves. As indicated in other chapters, the fetish of uniformity has been replaced in this design by a respect for the professional understanding in each school of what is best for its constituency. The concept of uniformity sometimes advocated on the basis of equal educational opportunities actually interferes with developing a program that is best for the teachers and students in a given school. The board of education in fact practices individualization among schools.

Relations between the individual school and the state department of education and regional accrediting associations are analogous to the school's relationships with the board of education. Obviously, regional accrediting associations and state departments should not use standard and uniform criteria applied equally to all of the schools under their jurisdictions. Their aim is to develop the best possible educational program in each school in relation to the community it serves.

As described in Chapter 14, evaluation measures show how well the school is achieving its own goals as approved by representatives of the state education department and the regional accrediting association. Conventional schools in contrast may cooperate only to the degree required to make a favorable impression. Such relationships not only discourage initiative, creativity, and openness of communication but may emphasize the importance of average mediocrity. The school as designed in this book constantly seeks improvements with whatever help the state and regional bodies may provide.

Services to the Profession

One other characteristic of the open school environment is the willingness of the school to share with other persons what it has learned about the process of change, what constitutes a superior program, how the results are determined, and how the school constantly seeks improvements. To achieve these goals, the school has an open door policy for visitors with systematic arrangements to help them observe the particular kinds of programs that they wish to view.

The school urges visitors to talk with students, teachers, and the supervisory-management team. An open school recognizes that it has nothing to hide, that some programs work better than others, that some problems have not been solved as they should and can be ultimately, and that at a given stage some difficulties are described as dilemmas rather than problems because they are not readily solved.

Relations with universities are indicated elsewhere in this book. Improvement of two-way communication means that school counselors and teacher advisers provide universities with better knowledge of graduates, their programs, and their needs. The school's more open environment facilitates visits, research, and constructive help from university personnel.

The school thus shares with other persons how it copes with situations. The people in this school do not assume that they have all the answers, that the rest of the world is all wrong, or that they have attained a zenith of perfection. They listen to visitors because other ideas may help. School persons explain in the clearest possible way what they are trying to accomplish and how it is being evaluated.

As another service to the profession, this *school for every-one* also provides some constructive solutions to vexing problems. Some individuals and groups are vigorously attacking today's secondary schools as summarized in the first two chapters of this book. The methods here aim to provide constructive alternatives to solving problems that others seem unable to cope with or to resolve. The plan here is not to give up on some students or some programs. The design possesses flexibility and alternatives in order to find solutions.

No Last Word

Since everybody's needs constantly change as personal and societal forces interact differently, this school emphasizes an open approach. When some program doesn't work as planned, alternative solutions are developed, recognizing always that most programs are good for some people.

The school that follows the philosophy of diagnosis, prescription, implementation, and evaluation seeks continuously to improve its methods and its products. Thus, students, teachers, and supervisors reflect an attitude of searching for better ways of doing things. They are open to constructive suggestions and urge people to make them.

No one is completely right or has all the correct answers; therefore, tolerance and understanding are always appropriate attitudes. Beyond mind-set, there are specific methods that work well in coping with problems, as indicated in the chapter that follows this one.

Some Possible First Steps
for School Persons

1. Using a sampling technique, find out what different kinds of persons outside the school would do: (a) to obtain information about a given subject such as number of failures, poor attendance, declining scores on norm-based tests, success of students in higher education or on jobs, and the like or (b) to try to change some school policy with which they disagree, or (c) to add some new program or eliminate a given practice. Then analyze the existing lines of communication from time to time to note defects, improvements, or other changes.

2. Collect all the news and other information released by your school or school system during the past 12 months—or a shorter period of time if you wish. Analyze the content under such headings as finance, curriculum

content, extra-curricular activities, personnel policies or needs, methods of teaching and learning, and the like. Classify the releases according to purposes, for example, to obtain more money, a better image, better working conditions for staff, better learning conditions for students, and the like. Analyze strengths and weaknesses in all the forms of communication, noting especially face-to-face interactions.

3. Use your findings for staff discussions about the kind of rapport that these programs provide between the school and specific groups.

4. Follow similar steps regarding the school's relationships with the other agencies and groups mentioned in this chapter.

5. Organize many face-to-face communications sessions in which the school persons listen more than talk—and aim to seek consensus on goals as described in Chapter 9.

For Parents and Others

1. The foregoing steps for school persons require your cooperation. Give your suggestions and provide help.

2. A problem in many communities is how to reach the considerable number of persons—both young and elderly—who have no children in school, therefore little knowledge of what the school does, and could do, to help them *directly*. When school people make appeals, these persons may resist for fear the result is only higher taxes. Organize special committees or group meetings of persons without children in school to hold constructive discussions on extending school services to such persons.

19
Coping with Problems

How does a school grow continuously? What methods are best to ensure progress?

Two statements made frequently are: "We have a problem" and "We—or somebody—should do something."

The first step in coping with an issue is to decide, even tentatively, whether the matter is really a problem or a dilemma. A problem by definition is solvable. A dilemma is not. A problem can be defined, alternative solutions considered, a single solution selected and implemented, and the results evaluated. A dilemma cannot be so ordered.

The educated individual distinguishes between problems that can be solved and dilemmas that have to be lived with, often unpleasantly. How one copes with dilemmas reflects to some extent the individual's effectiveness as well as mental and physical adjustments. The resolution of dilemmas certainly influences the character of an institution.

The person who spends much time and effort trying to solve situations that are actually insolvable only becomes frustrated. However, an institution that tolerates dilemmas can only appear weak and inconsistent. The effective remedy is to do something.

S-R, M, and DPIE

There are three basic methods for coping with problems and dilemmas: responding to stimuli; relying on memory; or utilizing processes that involve diagnosis, prescription, implementation, and evaluation. All three methods can be used by individuals and institutions.

The *stimulus-response* (S-R) process goes back to the dawn of recorded history. Although a relatively low level mental process, S-R is an essential activity for survival. Humans use it while driving cars, responding to fire alarms, and confronting emergencies. S-R solutions, however, are not the best way to cope with many situations that students, teachers, and school administrators face, many of which could have been avoided by better planning and preparation.

Memory (M) helps an individual or institution to react in relatively the same manner to a given stimulus whenever and wherever it occurs. Memory is a wonderful thing. It recalls advice and tells us where to find things. It helps us to keep from repeating mistakes. On the other hand, it can also cause unwise decisions when the new problem does not have the same elements as the old.

The process of *diagnosis-prescription-implementation-evaluation* (DPIE) is not new in education or in other enterprises. Without this process, science, medicine, industry, and other professions and vocations would still be underdeveloped. This systematic process for coping with situations is an integral part of the never-ending search for better answers in all aspects of human life and endeavors. The process may be comparatively simple or extremely complex, done in a relatively brief manner or over a span of many years.

DPIE Explained

Diagnosis is a process to determine the nature of a person, a thing, or a program through careful scrutiny of much relevant information. The focus is on preparation for decision making to improve the situation. The diagnosis may be self-diagnosis. However, in most cases it helps if the diagnosis is assisted by another, perhaps more sophisticated and certainly less personally involved than the individual is with the problems or the institution.

Diagnosis requires the availability of as much data as are reasonable to gather. Some of the data were discussed earlier in this book, especially in Chapters 13 and 14. Unfortunately, much data collected for school evaluations are relatively unproductive especially if the evaluations are made by individuals outside the school. Such outsiders may be competent, but they are not in a position to work closely with the students, teachers, and S-M team in taking ameliorative action.

The data collected for diagnosis are meaningful only if the persons involved in the school perform the diagnosis, with the help of other competent individuals. The function is to stretch the minds of those being evaluated so they will analyze better a variety of prescriptive actions that would likely produce improvements. The collection of data without diagnosis is a relatively fruitless endeavor. A diagnosis that does not explore a number of alternative actions is unwise, potentially dangerous, and likely to produce frustrations.

Students, teachers, and the supervisory-management team then need to explore alternative *prescriptions* that appear reasonable and might be undertaken by the various groups in the immediate future. For example, if students are spending little or no time in study and work experiences in the community, the *school for everyone* has available a number of prescriptive actions to correct the situation. Decision making regarding those actions involves students, teachers, parents, and the S-M team, plus action by the board of education and the central administrative staffs of the school system.

If teachers are spending much time watching and controlling students and little time in potentially more productive actions, they need to make ameliorative decisions among a variety of prescriptions that they or members of the S-M team might suggest. If the S-M team spends its time in relatively unproductive activities, the solutions may be found in reassignment of duties or addition of staff. The point is that as many prescriptive steps as possible need to be identified, then discussed thoroughly by the persons involved, and decisions made about what actions they should take.

The third action, of course, is *implementation* of the selected prescription(s). While planning the implementation stage, the persons involved should decide what additional data have to be collected for later evaluations. Most important of all is making sure that whatever is implemented has the support of the persons involved, that they are prepared, and will perform reasonably well what they need to do.

The *evaluation* stage, the fourth step in the process, requires data directly related to the agreed-upon objectives. The objectives, of course, are described in measurable, performance terms. The basic purpose is not to say that the school is better than another one, but rather to describe as specifically as possible what happened as a result of implementing the prescriptive action.

One finding might be that the evaluation was too soon and should be postponed before rediagnosis occurs. Evaluation that does not produce data for further diagnostic activity is relatively useless. The resultant evaluative decision on whether everything that was reasonably possible to achieve was actually accomplished should be made by consensus of all the persons who implemented the prescriptive action. Some compromises may be necessary.

DPIE is considerably easier today than it was in the past when data collection was more difficult and time-consuming. Schools today have the whole field of data processing

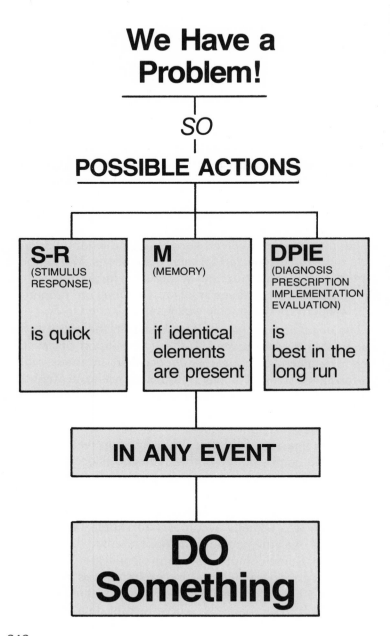

We Have a Problem!

SO

POSSIBLE ACTIONS

S-R
(STIMULUS
RESPONSE)

is quick

M
(MEMORY)

if identical
elements
are present

DPIE
(DIAGNOSIS
PRESCRIPTION
IMPLEMENTATION
EVALUATION)

is
best in the
long run

IN ANY EVENT

DO
Something

available to assist them in the task. Unfortunately, most schools have failed to take advantage of computer-based operations, often using them to print out the same kinds of student schedules, report cards, and attendance data as in the past, thus not producing as effective data as now are possible for diagnostic purposes.

Data processing, for example, may assist in monitoring more effectively the progress of students in learning, or the productive activities of departments, including the members of the differentiated instructional staff, and also the service and other activities of the S-M team. The printouts then are analyzed as a part of the diagnostic procedures in the never-ending search for more productive and satisfying experiences for everyone.

The message of this chapter may be the most important part of our description of what a school should be. Even though the suggestions and the processes are not new, the usual school fails to use them adequately. We envision an educational program based upon more systematic collection of data, more time for careful analyses by the persons involved, and better decision making based upon diagnoses and prescriptive actions. As those actions are implemented, the collection of additional and comparable data provides feedback of what is happening as a result of the implementations.

Again, the goal is not to say that a program is good or bad but rather to produce data for further DPIE in a never-ending, continuous process to improve the quality of what students do, what teachers do, and what the supervisory-management team does. The image is a school that constantly seeks to grow and improve by systematic means of coping with problems that involve the active participants. The process of change thus has a basis of sound priorities and procedures.

The Choice Is Crucial

Any problem may serve to illustrate how these three methods can be applied. Perhaps there is a sudden increase in vandalism or a rash of school fights involving dangerous weapons. Teachers, the principal, or the student council might utilize M (memory) as a technique for meeting the crisis, trying to recall how similar problems were handled 10 years ago or even one year ago. However, that solution might not work very well because of new conditions.

Another approach might be to use S-R: call the police, hire more guards, station teachers, student assistants, and school administrators in the corridors, or expel the culprits causing the problems. Any of these reactions may work temporarily to resolve the immediate crisis but they do not solve the problem.

Beware of simple solutions. A tough principal can do a policeman's job—so can a teacher—and create an aura of having a school or a classroom under control. But are those outcomes the basic purpose of education?

Emergencies may require police actions. Hopefully they will be done by persons with the type of special training that detection and enforcement requires. A recent metropolitan newspaper showed a large picture of a tough-looking principal in a long, empty school corridor. The accompanying article said the school was under control so learning was taking place. There were no pictures or words that told the story behind the closed classroom doors. Nor was the question raised about the possible use of trained law enforcement persons instead of teachers and principals. The diagnosis was inadequate and the recommended prescription questionable.

In the final analysis, DPIE *must* be utilized if any situation really is to be improved. This process, with various degrees of sophistication, is essential in the never-ending search for better solutions and progress in all aspects of personal and group living as well as institutional services and programs.

The final chapter of this book reviews and elaborates the total design for this *school for everyone* by putting it all together specifically in a brief summary.

Some Possible First Steps for School Persons

1. Recall several problems or crises that your school had to cope with recently. Were they resolved by S-R, M, DPIE, or a combination of these methods?

2. Take the solution to one of the problems listed under No. 1, or some other problem, that has *not* produced the results that you and others hoped for. Then plan more systematically, collect additional data, and follow the DPIE procedures that this design recommends.

For Parents and Others

1. The DPIE process is wonderful for coping with personal or family problems—with the comparable uses of SR and M as described in this chapter. The two first steps listed for school persons are analagous for your situations. Practicing these approaches will help you to understand better and help with the approaches to problem solving that school persons are using.

2. Apply the same approaches to improving your parent-teacher-student association or citizens advisory group.

Design
and Action

Total change is the goal. However, partial changes when carefully planned and executed represent realistic, transitional steps. Understanding all the relationships helps to clarify the decision making in each school. The leadership role is emphasized.

20

Combining, Selecting, and Proceeding

How does a school put it all together? If partial changes bring only limited gains that tend to disappoint and disappear, what changes will bring the new school into being? What process helps to make decisions on how to start? How is motivation to change maintained and complacency reduced? Who is responsible for what?

EVERYBODY wants to improve schools. The questions people must ask before starting are: how much, for whom, and in what ways? But agreements on answers do not come easily; differences develop around what to change and how to do it. Specific ways have been proposed in the preceding 19 chapters.

Two basic features of the *school for everyone* make its design unique. It has more options, broader in scope, than today's schools provide. Second, there are specific procedures for developing and monitoring the best possible program for each individual person.

What may you expect from this school?

The design provides specific standards for organizing, conducting, and evaluating a school. It serves as a basis for judging present programs in schools, planning and implementing future changes, understanding better why inadequately planned or poorly implemented changes are less successful than they could be, and for guiding long-term undertakings to improve schools.

Everyone in the school community needs a collective configuration to recognize the potential gains as well as the limitations of whatever changes a school community decides to initiate. The proposals are reviewed here to assist the selection, the planning, and the development of the local program.

Program-People-Structure

A triangle in Chapter 2 highlighted the three elements of the school that interlace with each other and with the learners: PROGRAM, PEOPLE, and STRUCTURE. Such a comprehensive design helps decision making to avoid the fetish of unnecessarily small or piecemeal changes that neglect important factors.

An example may help to illustrate the planning and action processes. Suppose a decision is made to place more emphasis on career education. First, reference is made to the chart on page 253 that concerns PROGRAM. The outline that goes with it calls for decisions on changes in *curriculum content, methods,* the *locus* of where the learning is to occur and *evaluation.*

Several questions then must be answered. So far as curriculum is concerned, which of the listed subject areas are to be involved? Which methods? Where will teaching and learning occur? How will pupils be graded and how will the total career education program be judged?

The next step is to plan in more detail, using the outline, *Program Elements,* starting on page *252.* For example, (Item a), what will be taught about careers in all subjects to all students? Or (under methods), will there be presenta-

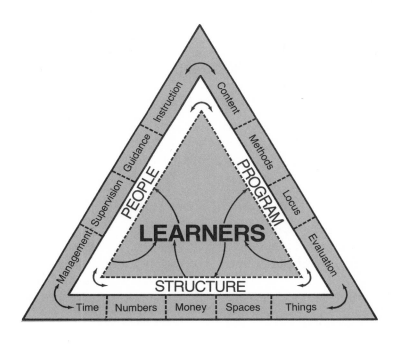

tions about career possibilities to all students? Where will career education occur and who will be the instructors? And so on. Note especially the elements under evaluation.

At the same time, the plans will consider the *people* who will be involved: the chart on page 257, and their activities in career education as outlined on pages 256-259. Also, simultaneously, the plans will include the *structural* elements in the chart on page 261 and the specifics under structural prescriptions on pages 260-263.

Along with these plans, there should be reference to the appropriate earlier chapters in this book where all of the foregoing items are discussed in detail. Whether the program selected is career education, improvement of basic skills, increased creativity, better discipline, changing report cards, action learning to make better use of the community, or any other aspect of schooling, this systematic approach will produce better results.

Let's review and take a closer look at the three components. First there is the PROGRAM.

1. Program Elements

The PROGRAM side of the model's triangle lists 19 aspects of curriculum content, methods, locus, and evaluation. Seventeen prescriptions for implementing the aspects are outlined for purposes of local decision making.

Program Implementation

Curriculum organization:

a. *Essential* learnings for everyone in all subject areas; *required* of all students.

b. *Hobbies* (special interests) that result when a student is motivated to learn *more* of the subject than is *essential*; studied in greater depth and/or to be creative.

c. *Careers* that are open to students who go beyond the *essential* and *hobby* levels.

Methods of learning and teaching:

a. Weekly *motivational experiences* (in relatively large groups) with presentations by teachers, pupils, outside persons, and audiovisual devices that aim to stimulate students to study more in each curriculum area than they think they want to do; required of each student during all years of school unless excused by the individual's teacher adviser.

b. *Reaction discussions* (in small-groups) where 10-20 students systematically gather to interact to the presentations, for further motivation, clarification, and develop-

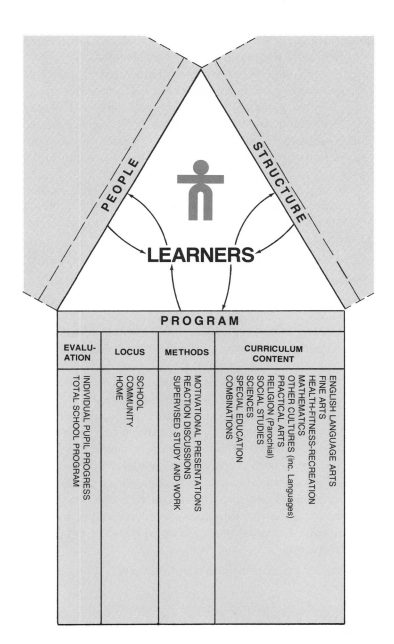

PEOPLE

STRUCTURE

LEARNERS

PROGRAM			
EVALU-ATION	LOCUS	METHODS	CURRICULUM CONTENT
INDIVIDUAL PUPIL PROGRESS TOTAL SCHOOL PROGRAM	SCHOOL COMMUNITY HOME	MOTIVATIONAL PRESENTATIONS REACTION DISCUSSIONS SUPERVISED STUDY AND WORK	ENGLISH LANGUAGE ARTS FINE ARTS HEALTH-FITNESS-RECREATION MATHEMATICS OTHER CULTURES (inc. Languages) PRACTICAL ARTS RELIGION (Parochial) SCIENCES SOCIAL STUDIES SPECIAL EDUCATION COMBINATIONS

ment of interaction skills with a teacher present to help them in these processes; required as under *a*.

c. *Supervised study and work* (independent study) individually or in groups, in the school, home, or community, following guides prepared by teachers, with a variety of learning strategies; emphasis is on pupil responsibility; applies to all students as arranged by teacher advisers and subject teachers in the various curricular areas.

d. *Continuous progress arrangements* enable each student to proceed at his or her own pace and individual levels of interest and goals; non-graded, with non-time-sequenced arrangements.

Locus of learning and teaching:

a. The *school* has a variety of study and work centers in all subject areas: silent for individual work; group study areas; special help areas; close supervision areas, and work areas in *every* subject field (shops, laboratories, gymnasiums, etc.). Also the school provides presentation areas for large groups, small areas for discussion, and study and work areas for teachers, their assistants, and for the supervisory-management team.

b. *Community* offices, shops, theaters, museums, etc., are used by students when these locations are better than the school can reasonably provide and when students can be scheduled there and supervised by school-arranged instructional assistants in the various locations.

c. *Home* facilities are used for those activities and those persons that can be scheduled there when the facilities are adequate or possibly superior to those in the school or community.

Evaluation of pupil progress (appraisal, recording, and reporting):

a. Periodically, the school reports to parents and others the progress of each pupil in completing the *required* segments in the learning sequences of all the subject areas, including cognitive, skills, and affective growth.

b. Comparative test scores, standardized or local, are reported to show how the pupil has achieved in relation to others as *based on various norms*.

c. What each pupil achieves *beyond the required sequences* is appraised, recorded, and reported, e.g., played on a team, completed a special study or project in given subject fields, participated in a play, or finished any other project not required of everyone.

Evaluation of the total program (school, community, home):

a. Changes in *pupils' learning* roles, attitudes, interests, behaviors, etc.

b. Changes in *teaching and supervisory roles*, productivity, conditions, accomplishments, attitudes, understandings, and related matters.

c. Changes in *community* (including parents) perceptions of schooling, attitudes, support, interest, and general productivity.

d. Changes in *utilization* of learning and teaching resources in the school, community, and home; utilization of money, time, spaces, and other features that influence learning, teaching, and supervision.

The program becomes operational as a result of the persons involved and what they do. Who are the PEOPLE?

2. The People That Relate to the Learners

The left side of the triangle refers to both professional and lay persons who have contractual responsibilities for working with learners. Parents and guardians are not included because all of them are not employed by the school system. The design, in fact, enhances their roles. A considerable number of persons who supervise students in the community are not included either. Their number varies from place to place. The teacher-adviser system and the more open environment of the school emphasize closer relationships and improved understandings with all these persons as described throughout the design.

The PEOPLE side of the triangular design for improving schools lists 14 kinds of persons in four categories: instruction, guidance, supervision, and management. Fourteen prescriptions for implementing each category indicate numbers of persons in relation to the number of students enrolled in the school.

People Prescriptions

Differentiated instructional staff:

a. *Professional teachers* are released from many clerical duties and routine supervision of pupils to provide time, energy, and facilities so they may prepare, perform, and evaluate better, advise students, develop curriculum materials, analyze needs and develop professional solutions, each according to individual talents and interests. The total number of teachers in relation to the total number of students is the range of 1 to 20 or 30, depending on local policies; the design recommends about 1 to 24-26 or so. Local financial support and expectations influence the decision.

b. The system provides about 20 hours per week, multiplied by the number of teachers in the school, of *instructional assistants* who help to supervise the study and work centers, develop materials, and perform other instructional tasks under teacher supervision; competent in the subject area, they help to supervise students and provide time for teachers to perform professional tasks.

c. The system also provides *clerical services* for about 10 hours per week, multiplied by the number of teachers, for use by teachers, beyond other clerical workers that serve administrators and supervisors.

256

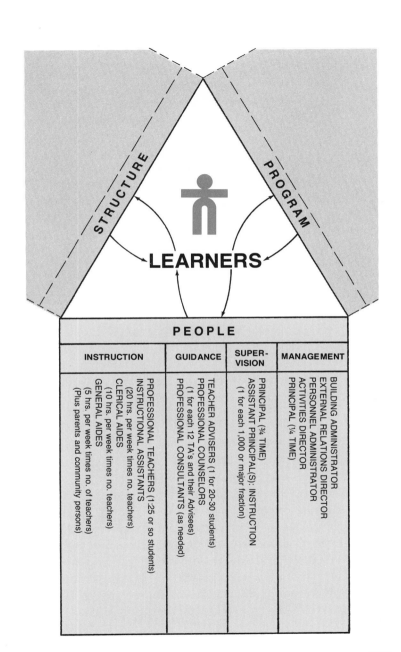

STRUCTURE

PROGRAM

LEARNERS

PEOPLE			
INSTRUCTION	**GUIDANCE**	**SUPER-VISION**	**MANAGEMENT**
PROFESSIONAL TEACHERS (1:25 or so students) INSTRUCTIONAL ASSISTANTS (20 hrs. per week times no. teachers) CLERICAL AIDES (10 hrs. per week times no. teachers) GENERAL AIDES (5 hrs. per week times no. of teachers) (Plus parents and community persons)	TEACHER ADVISERS (1 for 20-30 students) PROFESSIONAL COUNSELORS (1 for each 12 TA's and their Advisees) PROFESSIONAL CONSULTANTS (as needed)	PRINCIPAL (¾ TIME) ASSISTANT PRINCIPAL(S): INSTRUCTION (1 for each 1,000 or major fraction)	BUILDING ADMINISTRATOR EXTERNAL RELATIONS DIRECTOR PERSONNEL ADMINISTRATOR ACTIVITIES DIRECTOR PRINCIPAL (¼ TIME)

d. The system provides about 5 hours per week, multiplied by the number of teachers, of *general aides* to supervise the cafeteria and other areas and provide services not requiring clerical skills or special training in subject content, such as getting materials out and putting them back.

Differentiated guidance staff:

a. *Teacher advisers* monitor the educational progress of 20 to 30 students, helping each of them to change schedules to find and develop interests and talents, conferring usually on an individual basis, helping to solve "educational problems" and overseeing and reporting progress or the lack of it.
b. *Professional counselors* help students with personal problems, help teacher advisers to increase their skills in recognizing problems and referring pupils for counseling, each counselor working with about 12 teacher advisers and their 300 or so advisees.
c. *Special consultants* are used by both teacher advisers and professional counselors to help with difficult cases beyond the scope of their competences.

Differentiated supervision-management staff:

a. The *principal* spends three-fourths of his or her time on improving instruction and one-fourth on managing and supervising other programs.
b. For each 1,000 pupils, or major fraction thereof, there is an *assistant principal* who spends full-time on instructional improvement (also some part-time persons).
c. The *building administrator* supervises clerks, custodians, cafeteria staff, bus drivers, etc.—and the programs they involve—and also sees visitors and salespersons; the training is entirely different from the principal or assistant principal as is the case of the persons that follow.

d. The *external relations director* is concerned with local, state and federal finances and support, foundation, press, radio, TV, community groups, etc., with special training for these tasks.

e. The *personnel administrator* deals with police, juvenile authorities, pupil and teacher welfare, and oversees the differentiated guidance program, attendance officers, school nurse, etc., with special training along these lines.

f. The *activities director* supervises school clubs, social events, athletics and other performances, exhibits, and other "extracurricular activities." [According to the size of schools, items c-f inclusive are combined].

g. *Consultants* from the district or central offices of the school system or from state education departments, regional accrediting agencies, or universities help the school staff to improve the program but recognize the fact that the success of the school depends basically on items a-f inclusive as they work effectively with the instructional staff and others.

What people do and the effectiveness of the program are limited or enhanced by a variety of essential environmental elements. The third side of the triangle deals with STRUCTURE.

3. Structural Factors

The conventional school tends to allow time, numbers, money, spaces, and materials to control the school rather than to serve it. These elements not only are the easiest to count but also the easiest to change. Bodies that regulate schools emphasize these factors in accreditation for the same reasons. The public is often caught up in a similar syndrome.

School improvement requires that the structural elements become the servants of the *program* and *people* rather than their master. How the school administers these structural elements determines the effectiveness of the program and the utilization of human resources. The design indicates 19 prescriptions related to structure.

Structural Prescriptions

Time:

a. *Year-round school* availability plus continuous progress arrangements and systematic use of home and school learning environments provide students, teachers, and supervisory-management team members with much flexibility, under appropriate supervision, to plan the use of time for students and themselves in relation to purposes.

b. *Individualized scheduling* for students removes most control of time from the central office to the individual's teacher adviser who can change a student schedule anytime as interests and talents change. The office schedules only presentation and reaction groups.

c. *Teacher and S-M team schedules* also are individualized as decisions about who does what, and when, are made by individuals and their appropriate supervisors, thus changing conventional "loads" applied uniformily to all.

Numbers:

a. Pupils are scheduled into *large-groups* (40-100 or more) for about 30 minutes per week for a "presentation experience" in each subject area (eight in public, nine in parochial).

b. As soon as possible, or convenient, after the large group, pupils are scheduled into a *small group* of 10-20 for about 30 minutes for a "reaction discussion."

c. Numbers vary in *study and work centers:* 1 (alone); 2 (one teaches another); 3-4 (ditto); 10 etc. (interested in a

260

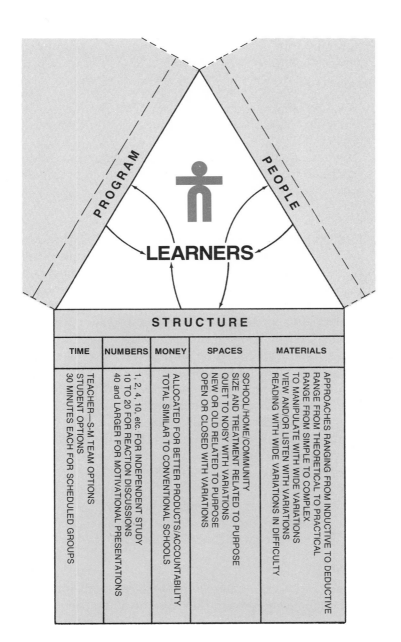

PROGRAM

PEOPLE

LEARNERS

STRUCTURE

TIME	NUMBERS	MONEY	SPACES	MATERIALS
TEACHER—S-M TEAM OPTIONS STUDENT OPTIONS 30 MINUTES EACH FOR SCHEDULED GROUPS	1, 2, 4, 10, etc. FOR INDEPENDENT STUDY 10 TO 20 FOR REACTION DISCUSSIONS 40 and LARGER FOR MOTIVATIONAL PRESENTATIONS	ALLOCATED FOR BETTER PRODUCTS/ACCOUNTABILITY TOTAL SIMILAR TO CONVENTIONAL SCHOOLS	SCHOOL/HOME/COMMUNITY SIZE AND TREATMENT RELATED TO PURPOSE QUIET TO NOISY WITH VARIATIONS NEW OR OLD RELATED TO PURPOSE OPEN OR CLOSED WITH VARIATIONS	APPROACHES RANGING FROM INDUCTIVE TO DEDUCTIVE RANGE FROM THEORETICAL TO PRACTICAL RANGE FROM SIMPLE TO COMPLEX TO MANIPULATE WITH WIDE VARIATIONS VIEW AND/OR LISTEN WITH VARIATIONS READING WITH WIDE VARIATIONS IN DIFFICULTY

common topic—or a remedial group) etc.; the numbers vary with purposes and locales.

Money:

a. *Financial input* is analyzed in terms of *product output* not only for purposes of accountability but especially for improving program and people.

b. The basic goal of not necessarily spending more money per pupil than do conventional schools in the same district is to *encourage better practices.*

Spaces:

a. Reducing the amount of relatively *unproductive spaces* such as corridors and standard-sized all-purpose rooms, plus the *systematic use of the community and homes* as teaching-learning environments, produce economies that in turn pay for better accoustical and visual services, additional equipment and supplies, and also for more specialized teaching and learning environments.

b. The size and treatment of rooms relates to the *specific purposes* for which the facilities are used.

c. Some spaces are relatively *noisy and* others extremely *quiet*, with graduations in between; too many combinations of the *extremes* are intolerable.

d. Some *existing* spaces in old buildings are utilized successfully with minimal modifications; *new* spaces should complement the old in meeting the requirements of the new program.

e. School spaces should neither be completely *"open"* or *"closed"*; a *combination* of the two, with *easy* changes as needed, is essential and more economical.

Materials:

a. *Study and work* materials provide for both inductive and deductive approaches to learning and teaching.

b. Materials range from *theoretical* to *practical* and are designated so that students know the difference.
c. The same as b., except dealing with *simple* to *complex*.
d. Ditto, considering the *wide variations* in manipulative skills among learners and teachers.
e. Provide *alternatives* to students who may prefer to view or listen instead of read.
f. Materials to be read should have designations indicating *levels* of reading competence required; wide *variations* of materials are needed in most schools.

Requisite Options

Some of the foregoing prescriptions are specific while others provide alternatives. The fact is that *a school for everyone* needs options for everyone—with competent guidance for helping the individuals in it to make wise choices.

At one extreme are some students who need constant supervision by a teacher and aides, the number depending on the size of the group. For example, a group of 30 such students needs a teacher and two aides who bring in other special teachers on occasion. The essential learnings and skills in reading, arithmetic, and communications are taught here along with the development of social attitudes and understandings. Professional decisions govern when and where students go elsewhere for physical development, fine arts, work experience, and other specialized programs. The central setting is like an enriched one-room school without the limitations of that bygone institution.

At the other extreme are the highly motivated, competent students who are largely on their own but still monitored by their teacher advisers. They have defined their goals and know how and where to reach them.

The school has a variety of programs for the majority of the students whose talents and interests are in between the two extremes. Each one also needs the individual attention that the school gives to the very able and the less talented persons.

The organization of schools-within-a-school is a promising transitional approach in schools with relatively large enrollments. One school in the building has few required subjects with much emphasis on the community as a learning place. Another groups students with serious interests in the so-called academic subjects. The fine and practical arts are central interests in another school in the building. The list could be extended.

These differentiated programs can be an antidote for the educational fads that pressure groups thrust on the schools from time to time for spurious and selfish reasons. Changes in emphasis occur but the presence of options makes adjustments easier while the total program maintains an essential stability.

Resolving the Difficulties of Change

Earlier chapters presented the need and the rationale for changes. However, when everything is put together as done in this chapter, the result can be overwhelming. Most existing schools cannot change totally at once. Newly organized ones have a better chance but even such schools have students, teachers, and supervisor-managers with conventional school experiences and ideas, some more so than others. Because of that, we have emphasized the need for options.

The model proposed here is an ideal. In a practical sense, ideal models are seldom completely realized. However, that situation is not necessarily true for *all* students and staff members. Some can make the complete change; others find those steps more difficult or, for the time being, impossible.

Schools are not static institutions. The idea of *not* changing a school is unrealistic. Some persons plead for the bygone days; others want to ignore problems, hoping they will

264

disappear or solve themselves regardless of what happens in the meantime. Such negativism is usually unproductive.

The emphasis in this school is on positive action. Schools are not improved by blaming university preparation programs, extremist groups in the community, the nature of the student body, the social mores, or by alibiing as some school administrators, teachers, boards of education, and other persons sometimes do.

Many of today's schools are beset by problems. As pointed out repeatedly in this book, there is nothing new in that situation. Suspending students, returning to the "basics" without recognizing what is important for different students at various times in their lives, or blindly reducing the number of years of schooling or the location of it without carefully determined rationales applied individually are overly simplistic escape mechanisms. The same may be said about such solutions as stationing the principal, assistant principals, or other guards in the halls or school grounds to maintain discipline without taking more constructive steps to alleviate the problem.

Some other schools today have fewer problems than were encountered a few years ago. Declining enrollments, less student activism and disciplinary problems, fewer teacher grievances, and more willingness on the part of parents are welcome relief to some school leaders. Unfortunately such developments can also produce complacency and continued ignoring of basic needs for changing schools to make them better and more productive for everyone.

The school staff needs to utilize problems regardless of the source as a basis for diagnosing and prescribing remedial actions. They also inform and involve members of the community, broadly defined, as a variety of actions are considered for implementation.

Who or what will bring the *school for everyone* into being?

Most changes in the past have roots in developments in the society. National emergencies, new technologies, requirements for economies, extra funds provided by governments and foundations, the urging and support of a variety of commercial and professional associations, and the like generate changes. All have impact for awhile. However, when the particular impetus stops, the new programs also tend to disappear, although usually not completely.

The school involved in the changes did so usually because of aggressive interests and actions by a few persons, typically a superintendent or principal, but sometimes a teacher, a board member, or even someone outside the school system. Always there is local leadership and motivation. If either changes, the program also changes.

The actions taken show the quality of educational leadership in a school. Some persons wait for emergencies and then take pride in coping with them. A few panic in the face of crises and require external help. True leaders constantly seek to improve the environment and the methods used to help everyone. The maintenance of continuous motivation to improve programs is less dramatic but more rewarding in the long run. It is also easier on everyone's nervous system!

At this point many readers will ask, what parts of the program do you recommend as a start? The temptation to give definite answers and recommendations is great but that response must be avoided, however, since schools and communities differ as do the individuals in them.

The author has no doubts about the rightness of all the recommendations in this book. They are essential in a school that truly serves everyone. How to implement the program in a given locale is the challenge of professionals in each school as they work more closely than ever before not only with each other but especially with the students, parents, and community persons.

Someone has to start the development of a *school for everyone.* That person could be you!

Some Possible First Steps for School Persons

1. Prepare a "motivational presentation" that indicates some local school problems that might be helped by changes in the program—without specifying what those changes might be in order to solicit more creative thinking.

2. Use this publication and/or the NASSP film, *Tomorrow's Schools: Images and Plans* or the filmstrip, *Whys and Wherefores*, to indicate the broad spectrum of possible changes so that persons in the audience have better backgrounds for decision making. Write to the NASSP for rental or purchase information.

3. Organize small groups to discuss and react to the various proposals.

4. Provide further facts and study materials related to areas of concerns and consensus that emanate from the groups.

5. Hold further meetings to arrive at further diagnoses, consensus, and decisions about what prescription(s) to follow.

6. Take the necessary steps to implement the decisions with plans to collect and report data for evaluating the results.

For Parents and Others

1. Ask school persons to meet with various community groups to study and discuss the proposals in this chapter, the aim being to seek consensus in planning support for school improvement.

2. Either individually or in study groups, collect and analyze the criticisms of schools currently appearing in newspapers, magazines, books, television and radio programs. Relate those criticisms to the suggestions for school improvement in this chapter.

Appendix

THE NASSP MODEL SCHOOLS PROJECT: SCHOOLS OF TOMORROW

The National Association of Secondary School Principals received a substantial grant from the Danforth Foundation in May 1968 to demonstrate in a group of schools the educational opportunities that would be enhanced when a variety of educational innovations are assembled and coordinated over several years with improved methods of program evaluation. The NASSP provided wide publicity about the grant and invited inquiries.

The original proposal was to work with seven schools. However, after many inquiries and visits to schools, a decision was made to include seven additional schools. Requests had also come from several districts that were starting new high schools and wanted to tailor them after the model; five such schools were included. Finally, later in the year of the selection process, an invitation was issued to designated districts to work towards the model in what was termed a "communications network." Fifteen schools agreed to do so. Thus a total of 34 schools participated in the project for varied lengths of time, most of them for six years.

The philosophy was to place major responsibility in the local schools for working towards the prescribed model. Therefore, the central project staff was unusually small in comparison with most other projects. Financial assistance to the various schools varied considerably.

The students, teachers, and administrators in those schools have contributed much to the present book, *A School for Everyone*. Although the ideas evolved over many years and from many sources, the experiences of the past eight years give the author much confidence in their validity and transferability.

What developed in the schools with respect to achieving the prescribed model for schools of tomorrow is told in an-other publication that shows what these schools found easiest and most difficult to change. A third publication reports illustrative data gathered by the school staffs and others to indicate how the programs were evaluated. A fourth, written mostly by principals who volunteered to describe developments in their schools, tells what happened and why from their vantage points.

The NASSP Commitment

Since its founding in 1916 the NASSP has been fortunate in staffing its national headquarters with some of the top professionals in the field. Each has had in-depth experience in schools and colleges and each has contributed significantly to the state of the art. Not the least of these is author J. Lloyd Trump whose influence over the past three decades has won him a permanent place among the country's leading educators.

Another characteristic of the Association warranting mention has been its willingness to re-examine the existing order and to probe for better methods of education. NASSP's strategy has been to build on the strengths of the existing system and faithfully follow Horace Mann's dual mandate: first, to continue those programs proved effective and in so doing to stabilize and perpetuate the society; and second, to serve as agents for constructive change. In this latter role Lloyd Trump has been both a stimulator and mover of people and their schools.

In *A School for Everyone* the author points out that in a society as diverse and complex as ours, no institution can effectively serve all people. In our schools most students respond well to what educators have come to describe as the traditional approach. Others require alternatives in non-traditional categories. The fact that we continue to have almost one million high school dropouts each year gives credence to the conclusion that the standard offerings simply do not meet the needs of all students. This book describes several viable and humane alternatives which appear to hold much promise for the future, and we commend its serious review to both professional and layman alike.

Fortunately, the goal of finding a better way is shared with a number of others. In this project the Danforth Foundation deserves substantial credit. It willingly and enthusiastically supported Lloyd Trump's quest for higher quality programs for the children and youth of the nation. NASSP's parallel commitment to continue in this never-ending search speaks for itself.

Owen B. Kiernan
Executive Director

CREDITS

Numerous persons of all ages over many years have contributed the ideas that generated this book. The most recent, of course, were the students, teachers, and administrators involved in the NASSP Model Schools Project, plus a number of persons who worked on the project staff.

The following individuals read an early draft of this book, making useful suggestions: Lloyd Bishop, Division of Administration and Supervision, School of Education, New York University; Lavern Cunningham, Executive Director, Public Schools Commission, San Francisco, California; Roxee W. Joly, Assistant Superintendent, High School Division, New York City; Edgar A. Kelley, Division of Secondary Education and Educational Administration, University of Nebraska, Lincoln; and Robert K. Lowery, Principal, Bishop Carroll High School, Calgary, Alberta, Canada.

Thomas F. Koerner, Director of Publications, NASSP, and Martha Christian, former Assistant Editor, NASSP, furnished editorial directions.

Melinda Padgett provided secretarial services.

William Georgiades, Associate Director of the project, and Professor of Education, University of Southern California, and I have interacted constantly in the preparation of this book and others growing out of the Model Schools Project.

The project and this book would not be reality except for continued support over the years by the Danforth Foundation, Gene Schwilck, President, and the National Association of Secondary School Principals, Owen B. Kiernan, Executive Director.

ABOUT THE AUTHOR

J. Lloyd Trump has been teacher and administrator for 30 years in both public and private elementary and secondary schools as well as in undergraduate and graduate university programs. The schools were rural and urban, ranging in size from 200 to 3,000. The university positions involved teaching and research, administration, and field services to schools. Professional association staff work, speaking, and consulting have taken him to all 50 states and to numerous foreign countries, including a six-month assignment in Pakistan.

His interests in educational innovations started in 1929 while he was helping to develop a curriculum for a new, consolidated 12-grade school. Teaching in one of the 30 schools in the *Eight-Year Study* in the 1930s added others. Consulting in the work-experience program of the National Youth Administration, with visits to all high schools in Chicago and the surrounding areas, highlighted the possibilities of differentiated staffing and other programs. A principalship in a large K-12 school in Gary, Indiana, a system with many innovations, provided other perspectives. Helping to direct a statewide curriculum program in Illinois and 12 years experience on the Board of Managers of the Illinois Congress of Parents and Teachers broadened his contacts with all types of schools.

The author has been a staff member of the National Association of Secondary School Principals for the past 16 years. Directing four nationwide projects, two supported partly by the Ford Foundation and two by the Danforth Foundation, involved many schools in a variety of projects. Working with numerous NASSP committees and programs helped further to crystalize *the school for everyone* that this book describes.

274